Tennessee Travels

1844-1847

Journal of Amos Hitchcock

by
Teresa Nyquist Tucker

© 2007 by Lily Lee Designs lc

Lily Lee Designs lc
Liberty Hill, Texas 78642
www.LilyLeeDesigns.com

For additional copies, call 512-355-9852 or
visit www.lulu.com or www.lilyleedesigns.com.

Tennessee Travels 1844 -1847, Journal of Amos Hitchcock
transcribed, researched, and written by
Teresa Nyquist Tucker.

ISBN 978-0-6151-3975-3

First Edition

Published by Lily Lee Designs lc
Printed by Lulu.com

Contents

Acknowledgements i

Preface iii

Part I: Introduction 3
      A. Overview
      B. The Colporteur's Mission
      C. The Transcription
      D. The Journal

Part II: A Chronological Journal 11

Part III: Visitation and Mailing Lists 79

Part IV: The Original Journal 87

Part V: The Hitchcock Family 179

Appendix 1: Publications 187

Appendix 2: Resources 197

References 199

Index 201

List of Illustrations

Bookstore Sticker	iii
Departure from Eden	8
Children's Tract, *inside*	24
Christian Almanac	43
The Colporteur	87
Amos Hitchcock, Ancestors and Descendants Chart	182
Children's Tract, *front cover*	188
Lyman Beecher	194

If it be so, be carefull that you do not gad up and down with your wife too much on horseback, or in Coaches; for fear it might make her miscarry. But you have learnt all these things well enough at the first, and without doubt have kept them well in remembrance.

Do but behold, in the mean time, what an unexpressible Pleasure your dearly Beloved hath in the tricking up of her sweet Baby in the most neatest dresses. What a World of pains she takes & spends her spirits, to make the Tailor understand, according to what fashion she will have it made; & to hasten him that all things may be ready and totally finisht against Sunday next.

O new Father, now open your eys! Behold what a pretty Son you have! How happy you are in so loving and understanding a Wife that knows how to trick it so curiously up in this manner! She was never better pleased! Undoubtedly the Summer nights are too long, and the daies too short for her to gad up and down traversing the streets of the City, that she may fullfill her desire of shewing it to every body: never was any thing more neatly drest. But the Nurse and the Maid with the Child in the mean while at Jericho; for their very backs and sides seem to be absolutely broken with carrying it up & down from day to day. And most especially when the Child is wean'd, and the Wet-Nurse turn'd away, the Maid cannot let it penetrate into her brain; that she now not only the whole week must rock, sing, dandle, dress, and walk abroad with it; but that she is upon Sundaies also bound to the Child, like a Dog to a halter; and never can stir out, as she formerly did, to walk abroad with *Giles the Baker,* or *John True the Tailor*; nor so much as go once to give a visit to her Country-folks or kindred; which occasions no small difference between the Maid and the Mistriss.

But good House Father, never trouble your self at it, for this belongs also to the Pleasures of Marriage; nor do not seem discontented because your Dearest walks abroad thus every day; but rather think with your self, she takes her spinning Wheel and reel along with her. And if in her absence, you have not that due attendance, nor find that in the house and Kitchin things are not so well taken care for, why then, you must imagine to be satisfied with th'assistance of the Semstress, or some such sort of person, as well as you were when you enjoied the Eighth Pleasure: You must also observe, that if the Child should sit much, it might get crooked legs, and then the sweet Babe were ruined for ever. It is also too weak yet to be any waies roughly handled; but it begins from day to day to grow stronger and stronger: Also with your Dearest carrying it abroad continually to visit all your friends and acquaintance, it learns by degrees to eat all things, and drinks not only Beer, but some Wine too. And I assure you it is no small Pleasure for the Father and Mother to see that this little young Gosling can so perfectly distinguish the tast of the Wine, from the tast of the Beer: tho when it is come to some elder years, perhaps they would give a hundred pound, if they could but wean it from it. But that's too far to be lookt into. And care too soon taken makes people quickly gray-headed.

Before you reach this length, yea perhaps before some few weeks are at an end; you will see this sweet Babe afflicted with either the Measels or small Pox; and then you'l wish for a good sum of mony that he might not be disfigured with them, in having many pock-holes. And it is no wonder, for who knows whether he may be past small-pocking and measeling when he is five & twenty years of age? But on the contrary there may then perchance appear so many glimps of marriage Pleasures from him, that such small things will not be once lookt at.

For if your Wife be now upon a new reckoning, and you come then, as I have told you before, to get a Daughter; you will in time see what a pretty sweet Gentlewoman she'l grow to be; how modestly & orderly she goes to learn to write and read; but most especially to prick samples; which perhaps she'l be wholly perfect in, before she hath half learnt to sow: nay its probable that she'l be an Artist at the making of Bone-lace, though she was never taught it.

Otherwise both you & her Mother will reap an extraordinary Pleasure in seeing your Daughter grow up in all manner of comly and civil deportments; and that she begins to study in the book of *French manners and behaviours*; and knows also how to dress up her self so finically with all manner of trinkum trankums, that all the neighbouring young Gentlewomen, and your rich Neeces esteem themselves very much honoured with the injoiment of her company; where they, following the examples of their Predecessors, do, by degrees, instruct one another in the newest fashions, finest Flanders Laces, the difference and richness of Stuffs, the neatest cut Gorgets, and many more such Jincombobs as these.

Nay, and what's more, they begin also to invite and treat each other like grave persons, according as the opportunity will allow them, first with some Cherries and Plums; then with some Filbuds and Small Nuts; or Wallnuts & Figs; and afterwards with some Chesnuts and new Wine; or to a game at Cards with a dish of Tee, or else to eat some Pancakes and Fritters or a Tansie; nay, if the Coast be clear to their minds to a good joint of meat & a Sallad. Till at last it comes so far, that through these delicious conversations, they happen to get a Sweetheart, and in good time a bedfellow to keep them from slumbring and sleeping. And it is very pleasing to see that they do so observe the making good of the old Proverb,

> *As old Birds did, the young ones sing, Which is a very pleasant thing.*

Happy are you, O you new Housholders, who have already possessed your selves of so many Pleasures in your marriage; and are now come just to the very entrance to repossess your selves of them over again; and perchance they'l never depart from you as long as you see the one day follow the other. Be not backward or negligent in relating your happiness to others; but if there be any distast or disaster that can happen in the married estate, lock it up in the very Closet of your heart, and abhor everlastingly the thoughts of relating it; then you will have many that will pursue your footsteps, and be Listed into your Company, & then also will your estate and condition be famous through the whole World.

Conclusion.

Thus long you have seen, Courteous Reader, how that those married people, who are but indifferently gifted with temporal means, indeavour to puff up each other with vain and airy hopes and imaginations, perswading themselves that all the troubles, vexations, and bondages of the married estate; are nothing else but Mirths, Delights and Pleasures; perhaps to no other end but to mitigate their own miserable condition, or else to draw others into the same unhappy snare; as indeed oftentimes hapneth. But it is most sad and lamentable, that the meaner sort of people, when they have thrown themselves into it, make their condition a thousand times worse then it was before: For they, who at first could but very soberly and sparingly help themselves, do find when they are married, that they must go through not only ten, but at least a thousand cares and vexations. And all what hath hitherto been said of the ten Pleasures, is only spoken of the good and most agreeable matches; and not of any of those, which many times are so different and contrary of humour, as the light is from darkness; where there is a continual Hell of dissention, cursing, mumbling and maundring; nay biting & scratching into the bargain, which for the most part is occasioned by the quarrelsom, crabbed, lavish, proud, opinionated, domineering, and unbridled nature of the female sex. Besides there are a great number (which I will be silent of) who do all they can to please others, and Cuckold their own husbands. And others there are that disguise themselves so excessively with strong Waters, that a whole day long they can hardly close their Floud-gates. So that you need not wonder much, if you see the greatest part of women (tho they trick themselves never so finely up) can hardly get husbands; and their Parents are fain at last to give a good sum of mony with them, that they may disburthen themselves of them. Insomuch that it is easie to be seen that they are in effect of less value then old Iron, Boots and Shoes, &c. for we find both Merchants and mony ready alwaies to buy those commodities.

Therefore O you that are yet so happy as to have kept your selves out of this dreadfull estate of marriage, have a horror for it. Shun a woman much more than a Fish doth the hook. Remember that Solomon amongst all women kind could not find one good. Observe by what hath befallen those that went before you, what is approaching to your self, if you follow their footsteps. And be most certainly assured that the acutest pens are not able to expound the light & feasiblest troubles and disasters of marriage, set then aside the most difficile and ponderous. Do but read with a special observation the insuing Letter of a Friends advice touching marriage; imprint it as with a Seal upon your heart; and lay fast hold upon that golden expression of the glorious Apostle, *It is good for man not to touch a woman.*

The End of the Ten Pleasures of Marriage.

A LETTER

From one Friend to another,

Desiring to know whether it be advisable to marry.

SIR,

I must acknowledge that the Letter which you have writ me hath given me some incumbrance, and made me more then three times to ruminate upon the question you propounded to me concerning Marriage; for it is a matter of great importance, that ought to be well pondered and considered of, before one should adventure to solemnize & celebrate it. Several of my familiar friends have troubled me touching the very same subject, and I gave them every one my advice according as they were affected; but methinks I ought not to deal so loose and unboundedly with you, by reason I dare speak unto you with more freedom and truth. First, there are two things which bind me strictly to you, Nature and the Affection; and moreover the great knowledge I have of this so necessary an evil. I will tell you my opinion, then you may use your own discretion, whether you will approve of my meaning for advice or not. For my part, I beleeve that of all the disasters we are subject to in our life time, that of Marriage takes preference from all the rest: But for as much as it is necessary for the multiplying the World, it is fit it should be used by such as are not sensible of it, and can hardly judge of the consequences thereof. Neither do I esteem any man unhappy, let whatsoever disasters there will happen to him, if he doth not fall beyond his sence so far as to take a Wife. Those troubles that may befall us otherwise, are alwaies of so small a strength! that he who hath but the least magnanimity may easily overpower them. But the Tortures of Marriage are such a burthen, that I never saw no man, let him be as couragious as he would, which it hath not brought under the yoke of her Tyranny. Marry then, you shall have a thousand vexations, a thousand torments, a thousand dissatisfactions, a thousand plagues; and in a word, a thousand sort of repentings, which will accompany you to your Grave. You may take or chuse what sort of a Wife you will, she'l make you every day repent your taking of her. What cares will come then to awake and disturb you in the middle of your rest! and the fear of some mischance or other will feed your very spirit with a continual trouble. For a morning-alarm you shall have the children to awaken you out of sleep. Their lives shall hasten your death. You shall never be at quiet till you are in your Grave. You will be pining at many insufferable troubles, and a thousand several cogitations will be vexing your spirits at the chargeable maintenance of your Family. Insomuch that your very Soul will be tormented with incessant crosses, which alwaies accompany this evil, in the very happiest marriages. So that a Man ought in reality to confess, that he who can pass away his daies without a Wife is the most happiest. Verily a Wife is a heavy burthen; but especially a married one; for a Maid that is marriageable, will do all that ever she can to hide her infirmities, till she be tied in Wedlock to either one or other miserable wretch. She overpowers her very nature and affections; changes her behaviour, & covers all her evil and wicked intentions. She dissembleth her hypocrisie, and hides her cunning subtleties. She puts away all her bad actions, and masks all her deeds. She mollifies both her speech and face; and to say all in one word, she puts on the face of an Angel, till she hath found one or other whom she thinks fit to deceive with her base tricks and actions. But having caught him under the Slavery of this false apparition; she then turns the t'other side of the Meddal; and draws back the curtain of her Vizards, to shew the naked truth, which she so long had palliated, and her modesty only forbad her to reveal: By degrees then vomiting up the venom that she so long had harboured under her sweet hypocrisie. And then is repenting, or the greatest understanding of no worth to you: Perhaps you may tell me, that you have a Mistriss, who is fair, rich, young, wise, airy, and hath the very majestical countenance of a Queen upon her forehead; and that these are all reasons which oblige you to love her. But I pray, consider with your self, that a fair Woman is oftentimes tempted; a young, perillous; a rich, proud and haughty; a wise, hypocritical; an airy, full of folly; and if she be eloquent, she is subject to speak evilly: if she be jocund and light hearted, she'l leave you to go to her companions, and thinks that the care of her mind, is with you in your solitariness; and by reason she can flatter you so well, it never grieves you. If she be open-hearted, her freedom of spirit will appear hypocritical to you: her airiness you will judge to be tricks that will be very troublesom to you. If she love playing, she'l ruine you. If she be liquorish and sweet-tooth'd, she leads your children the ready road to an Hospital. If she be a bad Housekeeper, she lets all things run to destruction, that hath cost you so much care and trouble to get together. If she be a finical one, that will go rich in her apparel, she'l fill the Shopkeepers Counters with your mony. And in this manner her lavishness, shall destroy all your estate. To be short, let her be as she will, she shall never bring you much profit. In good troth, I esteem very little those sort of things, which you imagine to have a great delight in. 'Tis true, if you take a Wife, which is ugly, poor, innocent, without either air or spirit; that's a continual burthen to you all your life time. The old are commonly despised; the ugly abhor'd; the poor slighted; and the innocent laught at. They are called beasts that have no ingenuity: and women without airiness, have generally but small sence of love. In these last some body might say to you, that one ought to take of them that are indifferently or reasonably well qualified. But I will surge a little higher, and tell you plainly, that that will be just like one who fearing to drown himself at the brinks of a River, goeth into the middle, to be the higher above water. You see now, why I cannot advise you to marry. Yet I would not have you to beleeve, tho I so much discommend it, that it is no waies usefully profitable. I esteem it to be a holy institution ordained by God Almighty. That which makes it bad is the woman, in whom there is no good. If you will marry, you must then conclude never to be any thing for your self again; but to subject your self to the toilsom will and desires of a Wife, most difficult to be born with; to pass by all her deficiences; to assist her infirmities; to satisfie her insatiable desires; to approve of all her pleasures, & whatsoever she also will you must condescend to. Now you have heard and understood all my reasons and arguments, you may then tell me, that you have a fine estate, and that you would willingly see an heir of your own that might possess it; and that it would be one of your greatest delights, to see your own honour and vertues survive in your children. But as to that I'l answer you, and say, that your reward shall be greater in relieving the poor and needy; then to leave rich remembrances to Heirs; and procure you an everlasting blessing, that you might otherwise leave for a prey to your children; who it may be are so bastardized in their birth, that they are both Spendthrifts and Vagabonds; for it happens oft that good trees do not alwaies bring forth good fruit. If, when you have seriously perused this my Letter, you are not affrighted at your intention; marry: but if you take it indifferently; marry not. And beleeve me, that a man who is free from the troubles & vexations of marriage, is much happier and hath more content to himself in one day, then another in the whole scope of his Wedlock. And what's more, a single man may freely and resolutely undertake all things, to Travel, go to battell, be solitary, & live according to his own delight; without fearing that at his death he shall leave a Widow and Fatherless children, who must be delivered over to the Fates, for their friends will never look after them. Hitherto I have kept you up, concerning your intention; and further I give you no other advice, then what by your self you may take to your self. If you marry, you do well: but not marrying, you do better. And if you will incline to me, rather then to marry, you shall alwaies find me to be

    SIR

        Your very humble servant

            A.B.

The

CONFESSION

Of the

New Married Couple.

THE CONFESSION OF THE NEW MARRIED COUPLE
LONDON,
PRINTED in the JEAR 1683.
Published by The Navarre Society, London.

The

CONFESSION

Of the
New Married Couple,

Being

The Second Part of the Ten Pleasures of Marriage.

Relating

The further delights and contentments that ly masked under the bands of Wedlock.

Written by *A. Marsh*. Typogr.

LONDON,

Printed in the year 1683.

To the READER.

Courteous Reader,

Thy kind acceptance of the First Part, hath incouraged me to go forward with a Second, which I here present thee with; being now indifferently confident that it will be no worse used by Thee then the Brother of it was: I hope there is never a Part of it, in which thou wilt not find somthing that will please thy Fancy: But for such as profess to be of the zealousest sort of people, and make use of the gestur of casting up the whites of their eys, when they intend to tell you a notorious ly, I would not have them to study in it, by reason it speaks a great deal of truth, and will not be so suitable to their humors; because it is a bundle of matter that is scrambled together, which could not be wrapt up in such clean linnen, or drest up in such holding forth *Language and pious hypocrisie, as such generally make use of: It is only fit for truehearted Souls that will solace their Spirits with a little laughter, and never busie their brains with the subversion of State and Church government: And being well received by such, it is as much as is expected by him who is thine. Farewell.*

The
CONFESSION
Of the
New Married Couple,

Being

The Second Part of the Ten Pleasures of Marriage.

INTRODUCTION.

It is an inexpressible pleasure for Travellers, when after many traverses and tossings too and again, they return quietly home to their studies and rememorates all the unexpected pleasure that they encountred with upon the one Coast, and the horrible vexations and confusions that they had upon another. And the very penning thereof, doth, as it were anew, repossess them of all the pleasures, and conveyeth them through all the Countries, without so much as the least moving of a foot. Just so it goes with those that have been under the Bands of Matrimony, and are loosed from them: These being then come to be solitary, at rest, and in quiet, can the more seriously rememorate and recogitate what pleasures they injoied at one, and what thwartings and crosses they met with at other times. And the writing down of these, doth not only afresh regenerate in them the received pleasures; but serves also for a Looking-glass to all married Couples, for them to recogitate what pleasures they have already received, and what joys are still approaching towards them. And for those which as yet know not the sweetness of the Nuptial estate, it serves for a Fire-Beacon that they may with all earnestness Sail unto it, and possess those joys also. Of those we have before demonstrated unto you Ten Pleasant Tables: But because the Scale of Marriage may hang somwhat evener, and not fall too light on the womens side, we shall for the Courteous Reader add unto them Ten Pleasures more, being that which some Married people have since confessed, or to be short with you, was formerly wink'd at, and passed over.

Published by The Navarre Society, London.

The First Pleasure.

The young Couple begin to keep Shop, and demand their promised Portion.

Till now, O new Married Couple, you have passed through the First part of your Wedlock with feasting and pleasures, and have injoied no smal delights in it. But what is there in this World that we grow not weary of? You have seen that the sumptuosest Feast full of delicate dishes, and the pleasurablest Country Scituations, with al their rich fruits, finally cloggeth, through the continual injoyment of them.

Nevertheless it is the generall desire of all persons, forasmuch as it is possible, to live in the World in pleasure and delights. Amongst the rest the gain of mony is none of the smallest pleasures, and this appears to be the least burthensom, tho it have much trouble in it. Therefore is it very much commendable, O young Couple, though you have a pretty estate of your own, according as your Contract of Marriage testifies, and as we have also seen by the Wedding you kept, your apparel, and the other ap and dependances, that you begin to meditate how to make the best benefit of your stock; and so much the more, because your Predecessors got it with a slavish diligence, reaped it together with sobriety, kept it with care, and finally left it unto you for your great pleasure. It is then also not strange, if you, as true bred children, keep it carefully, and make the best profit of it; to the end, that your Successors, when time shall serve, may find that they have had frugall Parents; and so walk in your footsteps. Verily this is one of the necessariest meditations in the World. If we could but any waies make the dead sensible of it in their grave, undoubtedly the Reliques of your Parents would rejoice at so happy and carefull an intention of you their children.

And truly, what is there, among other cogitations, more pleasurable, then to begin with a handsom Shop-keeping? For this through the daily gain, yeelds every day new pleasures, and by consequence a merry life. 'Tis true, Merchandize bears a greater respect, and yeelds also sometimes great gains;

but with these trouble somtimes, it is for the most part subject to great and weighty losses, which is the destruction of young people, and so intangles the merriest part of their lives, that fears and cares deprives them of their night rest. If the wind blow hard, they are presently in a fear that the Ships at sea laden with their Goods and Wares may be Shipwrack'd. If they will assure them, then the Assurer goes away with the profit: and they are also so greedy and cunning, that the least storm or bad tiding makes them very slow and circumspect; or if they be not so, it is to be feared, so there happen many losses, that then the Assurer himself might come to be lost.

But the handsom Shop-keeping is the surest and pleasurablest; for every moment you get new customers as well from abroad as at home, who buy continually with ready mony; or otherwise pay the old score, and trust the new. Yea all the news that goes about the City, is brought home and imparted to you. There's not a man dies, or woman brought to bed, but you have knowledge of it. Well then, what greater pleasure can there be then this?

Also, young Woman, you may, through love and care, herein be assistant to your husband oftentimes, which you cannot do in Merchandize, and so by degrees learn to understand the Shop, and converse neatly with the customers; whereby you can in his absence, also help the customers, and give them pleasing answers, insomuch that you oftentimes attain to as perfect a knowledge of the Trading, as your husband himself.

You are happy, yea ten times over happy, O housewively young Woman in this choice, and that not only for your husband, but principally for your self. For if that mischance might happen to you, that death should bereave you of your husband, you find your self oftentimes setled in a way of Trading, which you can manage your self, and set forward with reputation. Nay though you might happen to have children, you have the opportunity your self to bring them up in the same way, and so get a due, faithfull and carefull assistance from them, which will not so well be done by Men and Maid-servants, and over whom there is seldom so much command, as over ones own children.

And if your husband continue in health, and find that Trading grows quick, he perceives that by the assistance of his wife, something else may be taken by the hand that is also profitable, and then he will alwaies exercise some sort of Merchandise that is secure and advantagious.

It is most certain, sweet Woman, you will be the more tied to your housekeeping, and cannot so often go to visit and take your pleasure with your Gossips as you formerly did, in Coaches or by Water; as if your husband had taken any sort of Merchandice in hand; because that a Woman who is married to a Shopkeeper, is as it were also wedded to the Counter, by reason you dare not trust your Shop to old, much less to new men or Maid-servants, because they do not perfectly understand the Trade, and thereby also find occasion to make one bed serve for both and junket together; which makes no small confusion in the family; but little regard must be taken about that, for the importantest must alwaies be taken care of.

And be assured, if the desire of gain, small Trading, and bad paiment, begin once to take possession of you, the thoughts of all the former pleasures will remove, and you will exchange them for those that are more noble and becoming, *viz.* in the well governing of your Men and Maid-servants in the Shop and House, and taking inspection that they be obedient unto you; the Family must be wel taken care of; going to Market with the Maid to buy that which is good, and let her dress it to your mind; and every Market day precisely, with the Maid neatly drest, and following you with a hand-basket, go to take a view of Newgate, Cheapside, and the Poultry Markets; and afterwards, when your got a little farther, then to have your Baby carried by you, neatly and finically drest up; and in hearing of it, whilest it is in the standing stool, calling in its own language so prettily Daddy and Mammy. O that is such an extraordinary pleasure, that where ever you go, what soever you delight in, all your delight is, to be at home again in your Shop, by your servants; and most especially (when you have it) to be by your Baby.

And if you do get a fit to be gadding abroad with some of your friends and neighbours (for one cannot alwaies be tied as if they were in Bridewell, nor the Bow ever stiff bent) why then you have Ascen-sion-day, which may as well be used for pleasure as devotion. And if that be too short, presently follows Whitsontide, then you may sing tantarroraara three daies together, and get your fill of it. So that you may find time enough to take your delight and pleasure, tho you be a little tied to a Shop.

This being then in such manner taken into a ripe deliberation by some of the nearest relations, it is concluded on to set up a handsom Shop, and to furnish it with al sorts of necessaries; and by that means make that you may alwaies say Yea and never No to the Customers.

O how glad the good Woman is, now she sees that her husband, who is otherwise somewhat stifnecked, lets himself be perswaded to this, by his friends! and how joyfull is the husband that his Wife, who at first seemed to be high-spirited, is now herewith so absolutely contented.

O happy Match, where the delight and pleasure of both parties, is bent upon one subject. How fast doth this writhe and twist the Bands of Wedlock and love together! Certainly to be of one mind, may very well be said to be happily married, and called a Heaven upon Earth.

Here they are cited to appear who display the married estate too monstrously, as if there were nothing but horrors and terrors to be found in it. Now they would see how that Love in her curious Crusible, melteth two hearts and ten sences together. To this all Chymists vail their Bonnets, though they brag of their making the hardest Minerals as soft as Milk and Butter. This Art surpasseth all others.

Yet here ought to be considered what sort of Trading shall be pitcht upon. The man hath good knowledge in Cloath, Silk stufs, French Manufactures and Galantries, &c. But the Woman thinks it would be much better, if they handled by the gross in Italian Confits, Candied and Musk sugar plums, Raisons of the Sun, Figs, Almonds, Pistaches, Bon Christian Pears, Granad-Apples, and dried fruits; together with Greek and Spanish Wines, delicate Sack, Muskadine, and Frontinyack Wine; which is a Negotiation, pleasing to the ey, delicious for the tast, and beloved by all the World. And by this she thinks she shall procure as many Customers as her husband, because she hath familiar acquaintance with severall brave Gentlewomen, that throw away much mony upon such commodities, and make many invitations, Treats and Feastings. And she her self could alwaies be presently ready, when she received an honourable visit.

O happy man, who hath gotten such an ingenious understanding wife! that takes care and considers with her self for the doing all fit and necessary things to the best advantage. And really she is not one jot out of the way, for this sort of Merchandize is both relishing and delightfull, and must be every foot bought again.

Now the time requires going to market to buy Fir, Oak, and Sackerdijne Wood, and to order that the Shop may be neatly built and set up. And you are happy, that Master Paywell, who is a very neat Joiner and Cabinet-Maker, is of your very good acquaintance, and so near by the hand: He knows how to fit and join the pannels most curiously together, and so inlaies, shaves, and polishes the fine wood, that you would swear it is all of one piece.

Well here again is another new pleasure and delight! If all things go thus forward, certainly the wedding-cloaths will in a short time be, at the least, a span too little. O how glad you'l be, when this trouble is but once over! and that the Shop is neatly built, painted, gilt, furnished, and finely put into a posture.

O how nobly it appears, and how delightfull and pleasing it will be when this new Negotiant sees his Shop full of Customers, and he at one Counter commending, praising and selling, and one servant bringing commodities to him, and another hath his hands full with measuring and weighing! And his beloved at another Counter finds imploiment enough with telling mony, weighing of gold, and discoursing with the Customers. Then it wil not seem strange unto you, how it came to pass that your Predecessors got such fine sums of mony together, and left them unto you to be merry with. Therefore you ought also, even as they did, to provide your selves with a curious and easie to be remembred Sign, because your Customers by mistake might not come to run into your Neighbors Shops.

I have not yet forgotten that your Grandfather, being a Wollen Draper, first hung out the Sign of the Sheep, and his name was James Thomson, but by reason of his great custom, they called him, by the nick name, of James in the Sheep; which remains still as a name to the generation. And in like manner your wives Grandfather, a well customed Shopkeeper in silk-stufs, whose name was William Jackson, hung out the sign of the Silkworm, but his son going to school with another boy whose name was also William Jackson, for the making a distinction between them, they gave him the name of William the Silkworm, which also remains as a name to the

Family. This is not common only among the Londoners, but in other Cities and Country Towns, also among Coachmen, Wagoners, and others.

But come we wil take our leaves of these people, and turn again to our new married Couple, who can hardly rest quietly a nights, for the earnest desire they have to see all things accomplished, and their Trading going forward. And in time Tom Thumb got on his doublet, tho he was seven years pulling on the first sleeve. Yet before you come to this great pleasure, you'l meet with a troublesom obstruction in the way, which if you can but turn of bravely, it will be much the pleasanter.

For before the Shop is fully furnisht, you will see what there will be wanting to fill all the corners and places with commodities that must be sold by length of time, and to stand out the trust; and also with patience and meekness expect the coming of mony from slow and bad paymasters: therefore it begins to be time to speak of the promised Portion.

Uds bud, what a racket is here now! For the young mans father had made his full account that he should not already be dun'd for the promised Portion; not doubting but that the young womans lay all totally ready told of in bags; and thought to take it in the best sence, I will pay my son his interest yearly; and afterwards, in peaceable times, when there's little or no impositions, and that my Coffers are better furnisht, will then give him the principal.

And seriously the old man seems to deal herein very cordially, since other mens fathers do not do half so well, and only give this for an answer, *With young men must be promised, and with daughters must be given.* And others make their sons give them a bond, wherein he, as by example, acknowledgeth to be indebted to his father six hundred pound, whereupon the Father closes the match, and promiseth to give in marriage with his son six hundred pound: which at last comes to nothing at all, and only serves for a perfect cheat to deceive and hood-wink the eys of the pretended Gentlewoman and her Guardians.

It is no wonder where such Matches are made, if, when such things are discovered, there be a great deal of time spent, before they can come to the true pleasure.

But you, O new married man, who have a liberal father on your side, you can get provisionally your interest, and when times mend your principal. Perhaps it will not be half so well with your wives estate, for she it may be in her maiden estate, hath spent and run out more in gaudy apparel, to intice a Lover, then the interest of her estate could bear, insomuch that the principal is diminished, or the revenues thereof received and consumed long before they were due.

's Wounds in what a sweat and fear, with these sort of cogitations, is this approaching new Shop-keeper in! How earnestly he runs to her Guardians, to see if they will unriddle him this doubt that he is in. But to his good fortune, he finds it in a much better condition than he thought he should. For his dearest, hath spent much less in her apparelling and maintenance, then she could have done, so that there's not only mony in stock, but rents of her real estate that are yet to be paid unto her, though there was very much consumed for her Brides apparel and the other accoutrements. Well this is an extraordinary pleasure, and a great comfort for his panting heart. Uds life how many hundred kisses are now offered at the Altar of her sweet lips, that otherwise would not so much as have been thought upon. Therefore one may easily perceive that mony increaseth love very much; and that Lovers in these times are so bent upon mony, and so diligent in search of it, is no admiration; nay they scruple not to inquire of the Guardians, and up and down by unsworn Brokers, who negotiate with a very close intelligence in this sort of Flesh-Trade, and draw ten double salaries (and that ofttimes too from both sides) if they can but help anyone to a good bargain, and that he obtains access; and afterwards wheedle it about so, that it finally comes to be a match. But what sad issue generally such sort of Matches are attended with, is well known to the whole World.

You, O Lovers, who seek to be Livry men of the great Company, and aim to possess the pleasures of Marriage, have a care of the inchanting voices of these crafty Syrens, because they intend to batter you upon the *Scylla* and *Charibdis* where the Hellish Furies seem to keep their habitation. These are the only Occasioners of bad Matches, and such as raise a Scandal of that Estate, which at once affoards both Pleasure, Mirth and Joy.

But our new married Couple went clear another way to work, who now to their full contentment, act so many pretty Apish tricks, injoy such multiplicities of kindnesses, and toss each other such quantities of kisses, as if there were a whole Kingdom, or at the least a vast Estate to be gained thereby: So that they find, that in that estate, there are not only Ten, but a thousand Pleasures cemented together in it; whereof in the following shall be demonstrated in some part the imperfect gloss, but never the accomplished Portrait.

Published by The Navarre Society, London.

The Second Pleasure.

The Husband grows Pipsy; and keeps the first Lying-in: Takes the Doctors advice. Is mocked by his Pot-Companions.

Just as one Candle lights another, so we see also, that two, sympathetically minded, know, by the cleaving of their lips together, how to breathe into each other their burning hearts-desire, wherewith the one doth as it were kindle the other, and do every moment renew and blow on again their even just now extinguished delights.

Of this you have here a pattern from our late married, for whom the longest Summer daies and Winter nights fall too short to satisfy their affections; they hardly know how to find out time that they may bestow some few hours in taking care for the ordring and setting all things in a decent posture in their new made Shop; imagining that they shall alwaies live thus, *Salamander*-like in the fire, without being ever indamaged by it. But time will teach them this better. In the mean while we will make our selves merry with the pleasure of this married Couple, who see now their Shop fully in order, furnisht with severall brave goods, and a pretty young fellow to attend it.

But because Customers do not yet throng upon them, they find no other pastime then to entertain each other in all manner of kind imbracements, and to chear up their hearts therein to the utmost. Here it may be plainly seen how pleasant and delightfull it is for the young woman, because her physiognomy begins to grow the longer the more frank and jocund.

> *So, that to us, her countenance doth display*
> *Her souls content, e're since her Wedding day.*

But just as a burning Candle doth consume, though to it self insensible, yet maketh of hers joyfull by its light, so doth our new married Man, before few months are expired, find that he becomes the very subject of flouting at and laughter, among his former boon Companions; because every one jestingly tells him, that he is sick of a fever, that the paleness of his Face, the lankness of his Cheeks, and thinness of his Calves, doth shew it most plainly.

And verily there are some artificial Jesters who do it so neatly, that he himself beleeves it almost to be true: yet nevertheless, to avoid their mockeries, casts it of from him as far as possible may be. But his own opinion doth so clearly convince him, that in himself he ponders and considers what course is best to be taken.

But housoever as long as he goes and walks up and down, eats and drinks, he thinks that the tide will turn again. Yet finding himself inwardly weaker of body rallies with his own distemper, in hopes that by his jesting, among his merry Companions, he may from them understand what is best, upon such occasions, to be done or avoided; and they seriously jesting say to him: O friend, wean yourself from your wife and Tobacco, and drink Chocolate, and eat knuckles of Veal, or else you'l become like one of Pharaohs lean Kine. Oh ho, thinks he, if that be true, I have spent my reckoning this evening very happily.

Now young woman, don't you admire if your husband comes home at night discontented in mind, for his wits run a Wool-gathering, and he has walkt in a dump from Towerhill to Tuttle Fields contriving what's best for him to do, and how to compass the matter neatly. For to remain so from his dear and delicate Wife, not paying unto her the usual family duty, is below the generosity of a man; and to tell her what the matter is, is yet worse. To leave of Tobacco, and eat knuckles of Veal, is feasible. But to go to a Coffehouse and alwaies drink Chocolate, that sticks against the stomack.

Nevertheless Necessity hath no Law. And the Occasion overpowers affection. Insomuch that after a thousand pondrous considerations, he resolves to deny his dearly beloved Wife a little of that same; and to that purpose will somtimes in an evening feign to have the headake, or that he is very dull and sleepy, (which is no absolutely;) and thereby commands his man to call him up somtimes very early in the morning, as if there were forsooth Customers in the Shop, &c. and hunts up and down among the Chocolate Dealers to get of the very best, preparing it himself in milk, treating all that come to visit him with Chocolate instead of Tobacco; and he feigning that he hath an extraordinary delight in it; and on the other side, perswade his wife that he has a huge mind to eat a knuckle of Veal, some good broath, and new-laid Egs, or some such sort of pretty conceited diet.

But perceiving that this avails little, and that he grows rather weaker then stronger; away he trots to the Scotch Paduan Doctor, who immediately prescribes a small Apothecaries Shop, at the least twenty or more several sorts of herbs, to be infused in a pottle of old Rhenish wine, and twice a day to drink half a quartern thereof at a time: Item a Plaister to be applied to his Stomack; and an unguent for the pit of the Stomack, under the nose, and to chafe the Temples of the head; but most especially to keep a good strengthning diet, &c.

But this seems to have too much stir in the view of his wife; therefore must be laid aside; and away he goes then to a High German Doctor, who without stop or stand, according to the nature of his country, Mountebank-like begins to vaunt, as followeth: *Ach Herr, ihr zijt ein hupscher, aber ein swaccher Venus-Ritter; ihr habt in des Garten der Beuchreiche Veneris gar zu viel gespatzieret, und das Jungfraulicken Roszlein zu oftmaal gehantiret; ihr werd ein grosze kranckheyt haben, wan ihr nicht baldt mein herlich Recept gebraucht, aber wan ihr dieses zu euch neimt, ihr zold alzo baldt hups gecuriret warden, zolches das ihr wie ein redlicher Cavalier andermaal tzoegerust, daz Jonfferliche Slosz besturmen, erobren, und da uber triomfiren zol. Dan ihr must viel gebrauchen daz weise von Ganze und Enteneyeren, die wol gebraten sind, Rothkohl mit feysem fleisch gekockt, alte Huner kleyn gehacket, Hanen Kammen, Swezerichen, Schaffe und Geisse-milch mit Reisz gekockt, auch Kalbs und Taubengehirn viel gegessen mit Nucis Muscati; und Reinischer Wein mesich getruncken; es is gewis wan ihr dieses vielmaal thut, ihr zold wieder kreftich und mechtich werden, und es werd sijner liebsten auch gar wol gevellich zein.*

In English thus.

Oh Sir, you are a brave, but a weak Knight, you have walkt too much in the mid-paths of the Garden, and plukt too often from the Rose-tree, if you make not use of my noble remedies, you'l have a great fit of sickness; but if you do take it, you'l be very quickly and dextrously cured; in such a manner, that like a Warriour you may both storm and take the Fortress, and triumph over it. Be sure then to make often use of the whites of Geese and Ducks-Egs roasted, Red-Cabidge boild with fat meat, old Hens beaten to pieces, Cox-combs, Sweet breads, Sheeps and Goats milk boild with Rice; you must also often eat Calves and Pigeons brains with Nutmeg grated in them; and drink temperately Rhenish Wine; it is most certain that by a frequent doing of this, you will grow both able and strong again; and it will also be very acceptable to your dearly beloved.

Here stands the poor Cully again, and looks like a Dog in a Halter, and perceives that this Doctor Jobbernole gives him an abundance of words but few effects for his mony; because all his boasting, doth, for the most part, contain what he had before made use of; and is therefore unwilling to trouble his wives brain with all that boiling and stewing, and all the rest of the circumstances. This makes him take a resolution to let it take its course. But still growing weaker and weaker, is at last fain to keep his bed, and constrained to send for one of our own Country Doctors, and makes his complaint to him, that he is troubled with an excessive head-ake, weakness in the reins of his back, a lameness in his joints that he can hardly lift his arm to his head; together with a foulness of his stomack, which makes him that he can retain nothing, but is forc't to vomit all up again, &c. Out of all which reasons the Doctor perfectly understands the ground of his distemper; and in the absence of his wife, reveals it unto him.

O how delicately these Cards are shufled! if the game go thus forward, it will come to be a stately Pleasure! but principally for the Doctor, who privately simpers at the playing of his own part, and never fails to note down his Visits; but most especially if he have the delivery of the Medicins into the bargain; placing them then so largely to account as is any waies possible to be allowed of; which makes the Apothecary burst out into such a laughter, as if he had received the tiding of a new Bankrupt.

But go you forwards Doctor, it must be so, you have not studied for nothing; and it is no small matter to be every time ordering of new remedies; especially when we see that you constantly write.

  Rx *Vini Rhenani vetustissimi & generostssimi M ij.*

And then again to eat oftentimes Pistaches, Almonds, Custards, and Tansies, &c.

Though since the Patient, like making a Martyr of himself, is in this manner fallen into the hands of the Doctor, his dearly beloved Wife is not negligent to acquaint all the friends with it; who immediately come running to give a visit to the sick, and speak words of consolation to the good woman. But alas grief and sorrow hath taken such deep root in her heart, that no crums of comfort, though ever so powerfull, can dispossess her calamities: for the seeing of a husband who loved her so unmeasurably, and was so friendly and feminine, to ly sick a bed, would stir up the obdurest heart to compassion, and mollifie it with showers of tears.

But even as all the Relations, by messengers, are made acquainted with this sickness; report in like manner is not behind hand with making it known to good acquaintance and arch Jesters, who (as I shewed you before) are very ready to appear with their flouts and gibes, and instead of comforting, begin to laugh with the Patient, saying: O Sir, we have perceived, a long time since, that you were more then half your reckoning, and that your lying-in was much nearer then your wives; and we alwaies thought, because we had tasted out such delicate Wedding-wine for you, that you would have desired us to have taken the like care for to have such at yours, and afterwards at your Wives lying-in. Yet since it hath not so hapned, we hope that the Doctor hath taken so much the better care for it.

Thus rallying, they begin to get the bibbing-bottle, and guess at the same time, as if it had been told them, that the Doctor in his last receipt had ordered Rhenish Wine.

And just as the Women in the Eighth Pleasure of the First Part produce abundance of Remedies; the assembly of Men do here in like manner cast up a hundred Receits which makes *Peggy* the maid blush and be most cruelly ashamed at; but behind the Window she listens most sharply to hear what's told and confessed by those that be in the Chamber, as to the further matter of fact.

For Master *Barebreech* relates, that as he was travelling the last Summer into the North, and so forwards into Scotland, going through Edenburgh, met there with his cousin Master *Coldenough*, who look'd so lean and pale-fac'd; that Master *Barebreech* told him, in truth Cousin, I should hardly have known you; verily you look as if you were troubled; and I beleeve you have the feeling of a first lying-in through all your joints. Well Cousin, saies the t'other, it seems that you are deeply studied in the Art of Witchcraft, for I fear its too true. I went from home on purpose to take my pleasure for three weeks or a month, that I might store my self with fresh provisions, and sing a sweet ditty in commendations of my Betty. Ho, Ho, saith Master *Barebreech*, flatter not your self with such a fancy, that you'l get as much up again in three weeks or a month, as you have been running behind hand in four. If you'l do well, let's for a frolick go into France, there's a gallant air, and we shall be very good company together, and fear not but that we'l make much of our selves; then when we come home again, you'l find your self so well, and both you and your wife will be thankfull to me as long as you live for my good advice of taking this journey. To be short, the Cousins travell together, and Master *Coldenough* came home so lusty, fat and plump, that all his acquaintance, and especially his hungry wife, admired mightily that he was so fat and corpulent.

At this all the jesting-wags burst out into a laughter. But having toss'd up their cups bravely about again, Peggy comes in with a fresh Kan, and Master *Winetast* begins to relate how that he used to be familiarly acquainted with a certain brave Judge, who had a bucksom bouncing Lady to his wife. The Judge feigns a Letter, which at noon, as he was sitting at Table with his Lady, was brought him very cleaverly by his man. He seemingly unknowing of it, opens and reads, that he must immediately, without further delay, go upon a journey; having read that, prepares himself with his man forthwith to be going.

But whilest the Judge was gone into his Closet, as seeming to take some important writings along with him; the Lady calls his man privately into the Parler, and forces him by threats of her displeasure to tell her, who delivered him that Letter; with a promise of her favour if he spoke the truth. Whereupon the fellow trembling, answered, Madam, I have received it from my Lord the Judge; but he hath strictly commanded me to keep it secret, so that if he come to know that I have mentioned any thing of it to your Ladiship, he will have the greatest displeasure of the World against me. Do not you fear anything, said her Ladiship, but be faithfull in what you do.

A pretty while after, the Judge having been some time at home, and walking with his Lady towards their Garden, they met with a drove of Sheep, having but one Ram amongst them: Whereupon her Ladiship askt, Sweetheart, how comes it, that that one Sheep hath such horns, and the t'others none at all? My Dear, said he, that is the Ram, the He-Sheep. What, said she, are the others then all She's? O yes, my Love, answered he. How! replied she, but one Ram among so many Sheep. Yes Hony, saies the Judge, that is alwaies so, then (sighingly she said) alas poor Creature, how must you long then to walk some other Road!

There had been more related; for Master *Carouser* was entred upon a new subject; but because the Doctor came in, they were constrained to break of.

But *Ellen* the starchster, being busie in the Kitchin with the Mistriss about ordering the Linnen, having let the Doctor in; saith, Mistriss, the Doctor is come there, and is gone into the Chamber; by my truly Mistriss, I hear say that my Master hath got a fever. O Nel, saith the Mistriss, this is clear another thing, this sickness is not without great danger; and it would be no such wonder, if my husband hapned to dy of it; and where should we then find the Pleasures of Marriage that some arch Jesters so commonly talk of.

But kind Mistriss be not so hasty, it is impossible to express all the Pleasures so fully in one breath: you must note, that they are all as it were for the present hid behind the Curtains; neither must you expect to sail alwaies before wind and tide; and beleeve me there are yet other Nuts to be krackt.

The Third Pleasure.

Whilest the Husband is from home, the Wife plaies the Divel for God's sake. The Husband upon his journy will want for nothing.

It seemed to be a divellish blur in the Escucheon, and a cruel striving against the stream, that as soon as the Shop was just made and furnisht, then the good Man falls sick, and keeps the first Lying in.

Published by The Navarre Society, London.

But Experience having taught him, that with relishing and solid dishes a man may overclog himself; he thinks it not unadvisable, to take a journy now and then from home, to see if he can get some new Customers in other Towns, or buy in some Goods and Wares for his Shop; by which means he may as well take as good care for his health, as he doth of his Shopkeeping.

Yet what comes here in the way, the pleasure is so great, and their loves so tender and newly stamped to each other again; that the young woman thinks she shall do, as formerly *Cyana* did, either consume her self in tears, or drown'd her self in a River, if she must suffer this.

Oh, the whole World will be unto her as dead, and without any thing of mankind, if her dearly beloved depart from her! Well, who will not then but beleeve that the married estate is full of incomprehensible and inexhaustible pleasures and sweetnesses? Do but behold how these two Hony-birds, sing loath to depart! Yea, pray observe what a number of imbracings, how many thousand kisses, and other toyisch actions are used, before this couple can leave one another! Nevertheless the reason of necessity, doth forsooth conquer in a vigilant husband these effeminate passions.

Therefore away he goes, leaving his whining beloved sitting between her Sister and her Neece, speaking words of consolation to her; and using all arguments possible to enliven and make her sorrowfull heart merry; either of them striving to be most free in proffering to be her bedfellow, and the next day to keep her company: But alas, saies she, suppose ye did all this, yet nevertheless I have not my husband with me!

But because time and good company help to decline and pass away sorrow; she very happily begins to consider, that she hath now a fit opportunity, to invite her Neeces and Bridemaids and other good acquaintance, with whom she hath been formerly mighty familiar, to come and take a treat with her, and to drink a dish of Tee; for they have, when she was in her Maiden estate, treated her so many times with Tarts, Pankakes and Fritters, Custards, and stew'd Pruins, that she is as yet ashamed for not having made them some recompence. And she never could find an occasion that was convenient before, because one while she dwelt with her Guardians, and at another time with her Uncle; who took very sharp notice where on, and in what time her pocket-mony was spent and consumed, that they continually gave her for trivial expences. Which vext her so much the more, because the treat she received, was for the most part done, to bring her acquainted with this or that Gentlewomans Brother, or Cousin, or some other pretty Gentlemen; to the end, that by this means she might happen to make a gallant Match; and indeed the first original of the wooing, and acquaintance with her beloved, had there its foundation.

To treat these Gentlewomen when her husband is at home, would no waies appear so well; and so much the more, because they generally suffer themselves to be conducted to the place by one or other of their Gallants; who then either very easily are persuaded, or it may be of themselves, tarry to take part with them. Therefore this must be done and concluded on, because she hath now the disposal and keeping of the mony as well as her husband.

Here now must *Doll* run up and down tan-twivy to borrow a Rowling-pin, and some other new invented knick-knacks, to bake Cheesekakes and Custards in; whilest *Mage* is also hardly able to stand longer upon her legs, with running up and down to fetch new-laid Egs, Flour, Sugar, Spices, blanch'd Almonds, &c. The Mistriss and *Doll* are able to perform this duty well enough; for they both helpt to do it, very neatly at her Neeces birth-day; but the Pastry-Cook must be spoken to for the making a delicate minc'd Py; and *Mage* must run to the Confit-makers in *Black-Fryers*, to fetch some Conserves, Preserves, and of all other sorts of Sweetmeats, Raisins of the Sun, and more of the like ingredients, &c. for she knows best where all those things are to be had. And for a principal dish there ought to be a Pot of Venison, a couple of Neats-tongues, a delicate peece of Martelmas beef, some Anchovis, and Olives for the Gentlemen, because they certainly will accompany the Gentlewomen. And truly they that bring them, may very well tarry to carry them home again; it is also but one and the same trouble. Goodman Twoshoes is gone out of Town, and sees it not, neither need he know it when he comes home: He treats so many of his friends and acquaintance, and then again next day following invites them to a Fish-dinner. I may very well play my part once in my life, and have all things to my mind, let come on't what will, who knows whether such another occasion may happen again this three years. And against next morning, very privately, she invites the Gentlewomen alone, to come about nine a clock in the morning, to eat hot Buns, and Cakes, for then they come precisely out of the Oven; and in the afternoon again, to some curious Fruit, Pankakes and Fritters, and a glass of the purest Canary let it cost n'er so much, or be fetcht ne'r so far.

Thus runs the tongue of this pretty housewife, that but a while ago was so sorrowfull for the departure of her beloved husband. Certainly there's nothing comes out more suddenly, or dries up more easily, then womens tears!

But hangt no more of that; for the guests will be here presently, therefore all things ought to be in order for mirth. And moreover there there are some of them that frequent Mr. Baxter's Puritanical Holding-forth, whose heads will immediately, in imitation of their Patron, hang like Bull-rushes; for they are taught to mourn with the sorrowfull, and to rejoice with the joifull. But it is now a time to be merry, and throw away masks and vizards; for all is done under the Rose, and among good acquaintance. And verily if the good woman had not this or some such sort of delight, where should we find the pleasures of marriage? for in the first Lying-in of the husband there was no looking for them.

Come on then, that mirth may be used, let the Cards also be brought in sight; which formerly, out of a Puritanical humour, ought not to have been seen in a house; nay, not so much as to have been spoken of; but now every one knows how to play artificially at Put, all Fours, Omber, Pas la Bete, Bankerout, and all other games that the expertest Gamesters can play at. And who knows whether they do not carry in their Pockets, as False-Gamesters do, Cards that are cut and marked. They learn to play the game at Bankerout so well with the Cards, that in a short time they can and also do it with their Housholdstuf, Wares, and Commodities. To be sure, you'l alwaies find, that every one of them, by length of time, are capable of setting up a School, and to act the part of a Mistriss. And most especially they learn to discourse very exactly touching the use and misuse thereof; just as these dissimulating Wigs intend to do, though indeed men have never seen that they practised this lesson themselves.

But, although the Mistriss and her Companions know little or nothing of these tricks, they serve howsoever, without setting up a School, and that also for nothing, for good Instructresses to their servants, who hereby are most curiously taught, what paths they have to walk in, and what's best for them to do that they may follow their Mistresses footsteps, as soon as their Master and Mistriss are but gone abroad together; who then know so exactly how to dance upon those notes, that we thought it necessary, as being one of the principallest Pleasures of Marriage, also to be set down in the Third Table of the First Part.

Many women, who are sick of this liquorish and sweet-tooth'd disease, will be grumbling very much at this, that such a blame and scandal should be cast upon their innocent sex; and say that Batchelors hereby will be afraid to marry; But if they, and the Gentlewomen that were in private domineering together, had not gone to Confession, and made a publick relation of it, who would have known it. Therefore this sort of well treated female Guests, are like unto those that when they have gotten a delicate bit by the by, cannot fare well but they must cry roast-meat, though they should be beaten with the spit for it.

But the good ones, though they are thin sown, who are not distempered with this evil, never trouble themselves at what one will say, or another write concerning women, because their guiltless consciences, serves them as well as a thousand witnesses; and they are very indifferent whether that the deceased scandal raiser Hippolitus do arise, and come into the World again; daring him in this manner

> *Surge then Hippolytus, out from thy Ghostly nest:*
> *Who scandal least esteem, revenge themselves the best.*

Yet howsoever though this is true, nevertheless I must furnish the delicate stomackt Ladies with some sort of weapons, that they may be in a posture of defending themselves against their vituperous enemies: For verily there are several men that walk not so even and neat in their waies as they ought to do; and who knows, whether our Mistresses dearly Beloved, at this very present, doth not as many others have done; who when they are travelling any whither, the first thing they do, is to be very diligent, and look earnestly about, whether there be not some handsom Gentlewoman that travels with them, by whom they very courteously take place, shewing themselves mightily humble and complacent, and telling them that they are Batchelors or at the least Widowers; then casting out a discourse of playing a game at Cards, that they may the better see what mettle the Lady is made of, and then again when they come to a Baiting-place, or where they must stay the night over, there they domineer lustily with them, and play the part of a Rodomontade. Where many times more is acted and spent, then they dare either tell their Wives, or their father Confessors of.

Others there are, who seek not so much such company, but very artificially before hand, know how to find out such Fellow-travellers as most suit with their own humour; to that end providing themselves with some Bottles of Canary, and pure Spanish Tobacco; and where ever they come are sure to make choice of the best Inn, where there's a good Table, delicate Wine, (and a handsom Wench) to be had.

Certainly, if the Husband thus one way, and his Wife another, know how to find out the Pleasures of Marriage, they are then both of them happy to the utmost. Is it not possible, but that they might, if this continued long, take a journy, for pleasure, to Brokers-Hall? For at first it was by them esteem'd too mean a place to be look'd upon, and not worth their thinking of: but then its probable it may come into their considerations, by reason that rents are low there, provisions very cheap, and pleasures in abundance; neither hath Pride or Ambition taken any habitation there. Nay, who knows but that they might chance to observe that there is no such need of feasting and junketting; nor be subject to so many visits, because there dwells not such a number of their friends and acquaintance: and besides all this, you may there, for a small matter, agree with the Collectors of the Excises, so that, for a whole year, you may have Wine, and severall other things plenty, for little or nothing.

But let's lay aside all this, because they are untimely cogitations, that fly astray; and it is much decenter that we turn again to our kind-hearted Mistriss, with her merry companions; who now, are about the taking leave of each other; using, to shew their gratitude, whole bundles full of complements; offering them up with an inexpressible amiablenes and eloquency for the respect and honour they have received; and confirm them with so many kisses, cursies, bows and conges, that it is easie to be perceived, that on both sides its cordially meant. And Doll, that good and faithfull servant, is not able to express how pleasing this entertainment hath been to all the company. Nay, it lies buzzing her so in the pate, that she cannot be at quiet in a morning, whilest her Mistriss is asleep, but she must, with the Neighbors Maids, either at the opening of the Shop, or sweeping of the street, be tatling and telling of it to them; putting, every foot, into their hands privately, some Almonds and Raisins, that came in by *leger de main*: Relating unto them, as if she did it by a scrole, what a horrible quantity of things she hath to scour and wash, that must be made clean, and set in order, against the time that the Bridemaids, as it was mentioned, are to come again alone; and so much the more, because her Master is daily expected home. Who then finally coming in, is not ordinarily welcomed, for she is so full of joy that her husband is come home, that both her tongue and actions are incapable of demonstrating her felicity; and he on the t'other side, is so glad to find his dearly Beloved in good health, and all things in decent order, that it is beyond imagination.

All this while they both laugh in their sleeves, that each one, in th'absence of the t'other, hath taken to themselves such a private an cunning pleasure. Finding so much content and injoiment therein, that they both hope to serve themselves again with the like occasion. O mighty Pleasure of Marriage! Who would not but be invited to go into this estate? Especially if we proceeded to write down and rehearse the further Confession of the separate Pleasures of Man and Wife, which is preserved as matter for the insuing Fifth and Sixth Pleasure.

The Fourth Pleasure.

The Wife will be Master of the Cash, or mony Chest.

As Mony is one of the most curiousest Minerals, is it, in like manner, the less admirable, that the handling and use there of rendreth the greatest Pleasures of the World. It is Loves Fire, and Charities Fountain. Yea, if Man and Wife in their house keeping may be esteemed or compared to the Sun and Moon in the Firmament; verily, those merry white or yellow boies, may very well be considered of as twinkling stars.

It rejoiceth all mankind to behold in the sky the innumerable multitude of glittering Stars: but it is a far surpassinger Pleasure, that the new married Couple receive, when they see vast heaps of Silver and Gold ly dazling their eys, and they Lording over it.

You, O lately married Couple, possess this Pleasure to the utmost; you have to your content received your promised Portions; you onely want the great Iron Mony-Chest to lock it up in securely, and to keep it safely, that it may be laid out to advantage. O how pleasant the free dispensation thereof is unto you! What a noble Valley it is to walk in between these Mountains, and to delight your eys with such an object!

Yet nevertheless, O faithfull Couple, here is need that a great deal of prudence be used, as well in the laying of it out, as the preserving of it. In ancient times it hath been often observed and taken notice of, that where mony was hid, the places were generally hanted with terrible spirits, and strange Ghosts, that walked there, coming in frightfull apparitions: but since they have been driven out of our Country and Houses; there's another sort of Imp come in, ten times wickeder then any of the other; which regards nor cares neither for Crosses, Holy-water, Exorcisms, or any sort of Divel-drivers; but dares boldly shew himself at noon-day, namely a Plague-Divel, which sets Man an Wife together by the ears, to try who of them both shall have the command and government of the Cash or mony-box.

And to the end he may herein act his Part well, he knows how very subtlily first to fill the weak womans ears full, that she ought above all things to have the command of the cash; because she had such a great Portion; and that it is her mony which she hears gingle so. And then again, because the care of the house-keeping is appropriated to be her duty, it is against all reason, that she, like a servant, should give an account to her husband, what, wherefore, or how that the mony is laid out; because the necessaries also for house-keeping are so many, that they are without end, name or number, and it is impossible that one should relate or ring them all into the ears of a Man. Likewise the good woman cannot have so fit an occasion every foot to be making some new things, that she may follow the fashion, as it is usual for women to do; much less to have any private pocket-mony, to treat and play the Divel for God's sake, with her Bride-Maids, when her husband is gone from home.

And on the contrary, when men pay out any thing, it goes out by great sums, according as is specified by the accounts delivered, which must be set to book, and an acquittance given: This cannot be so done with every pittifull small thing that belongs to house-keeping. Insomuch that the Husband can then, with all facility, demand what Mony is needful for his occasion from his Wife.

Moreover, when the Wife hath the command of the mony, she can alwaies see in what condition and state her affairs stands; and by taking good observation thereof, her husband cannot fob her off with Pumpkins for Musmillions; but she'l easily perceive whether she be decreasing or increasing in her estate. So that if her husband might come to dy, and she be left a Widow with several children, she can immediately see and understand in what posture her affairs stands, and whether she be gotten forward or gone backward in the World.

And what's more yet, it would be a great shame for a Woman, who hath alwaies been so highly respected by her husband; and as it appeared to all the World, was honoured like a Princess; that she should within dores be as servile as a servant; and must be fed out of her husbands hands, just as if she were a wast-all, a sweet-tooth, or gamestress, &c.

The Fifth Pleasure.

Of Mens negligence of their affairs; whereby their Antic-tricks and loss of time is discovered.

Verily the Women, being the weakest Vessels, are many times most cruelly impeacht, when the Marriage-Ship sails not well before Wind and Tide: just as if they, to whom is only given the charge of the Family, care of the Kitchin, and nourishment of the Children, were the occasioners of sad casualities and disasters in the Merchandizes and Shop-keepings: When, on the contrary, the negligence of the Men is many times so great, that if the Woman knew not how to carry her self like a prudent *Abigail*, it would be impossible ever to bring the Ship to a safe harbour, and to free it from Shipwrack, but all things must run to a total destruction.

Many men are free hereof, who are continually using their utmost indeavours, and take their chiefest delight in the promotion of their affairs, by day with their bodies, and at night with their sences, are earnestly busie in contriving them it. Whose main aim is, to live honestly, to get a good name, to shew good examples to their Children and Servants, to leave somthing to their Widows, and never to be a laughing-stock or derision to their enemies. And this manner of diligence makes no labour irksom, no morning too early, nor no evening too late for them.

But others, on the contrary, are so easie humoured, and so negligent of their vocation, that they think its much below the respect of a Man, to be seen whole daies in their houses with their Wives, and about their affairs. Then in such cases, there must, by every one in his calling, be found a multitude of lame excuses, before they can blind the eys of a quick-sighted Woman, or pin it upon her so far, that she perceives not he seeks his pleasure from her, in whom his whole delight ought to be.

If it be *Doctor of Physick*, he forsooth hath no time to study, because he must go to visit a Patient that hath a violent Ague, to see what operation the

Cordial hath done which he ordered him to take yesternight; for if any thing else should come to it, he would certainly be a dead man, &c.

And if you do but trace his paths and Patient, it is by his friend, who yesternight was troubled with a vehement Cellar-Fever; and at the very last, before he went to sleep, took in a swinging bowl of strong liquor; which made his Pulse beat so Feaverish and disorderly the next morning, that he was necessitated, at one draught, to whip off a lusty glass of Wormwood-Wine, (an excellent remedy for the Ague;) and then to walk an hour or two upon it, wherein the Doctor accompanying him, it causes the better operation.

Here now you see the Doctor, and what Ague the Patient hath, what he takes for't, what comes to it, and how dead a man he is. Truly the Doctor hath made as neat a guess at it, as if he had studied long for it. Hang the Books, when a man hath his Art so perfect in his Pate.

For this, the Doctor hath so much good again, when he hath a mind to visit a Patient in Tuttle-street, or St. Jameses Square, this Patient walks along with him for company. And when one hand washes the other in this manner, O then they are both so Silver clean!

Turn you about now to the *Counsellors*, and see how their Studies are all on Fire, only to be going too and again from one Court to another, to hear, forsooth, this or t'other Cause pleaded, that mightily concerns them, thereby to take their measures accordingly: When to the contrary, it serves to no other purpose then to sell a parcel of Chatwood, and tatle tales, of some brave Practitioners, a great deal worse then women would do; and finally to appoint a place, where in the evening they may accompany their Fraternity at a good glas of Wine.

Under this bundle resorts continually the Shittlecock Excisemen, accompanied with Collectors and Promooters, who are the greatest Bellringers in Taverns, and somtimes, in one evening, spend as much in Rhenish Wine, Oisters and Tobacco; as ten sufficient Families would do in a month. These live without care, and command freely out of a full purse, imagining in themselves that all the Revenues are their own. And if their Wives do, in the least, but peep into their concerns; they presently baptize it with the name of going upon an exploit, to chase a fat Doe, or neatly to attrap some Defrauder. And that this part may have the better gloss, when they come home in the morning, they have their pockets full of mony, which they throw into their wives laps; and tell them that they have attrapped some body, and agreed with them for a great sum of mony, having in part of paiment received this; when to the contrary, it is all the King and Countries mony, only taken out of their Offices. This generally lasts so long, till they are pursued by the Treasurer, and are arrested, and clapt up, or that they prevent it by playing Bankrupt, and in this manner leave a sorrowfull Widow and Children behind them.

By these the Foolwise *Notary's* for the most part join themselves; making their Wives beleeve that they are sent for into this or t'other Alehouse or Tavern, about an Excise-mans business; or to write a Will, or a Contract of agreement of Merchandize; though it be to no other end or purpose then to have a perfect knowledge who plaies best at Ticktack, Irish, Backgammon, Passage, or All-fours. From thence then they cannot come before it be late in the night, and have learnt there to make a Scotch Will so wel, that they are, by two witnesses, half carried, and half trail'd home to their houses; bragging still, that they have had Wine and Beer, and received mony into the bargain. Thus all things is baptized with the name of having earnest business.

The like knowledge have also the *Merchants*, *Shop-keepers*, and others who love company, to alledge for their excuses and defence; but the most fashionable, give it the name of going to a sale of some Lands and Houses, Parts of Ships, Merchandizes, Shop-Wares, Meetings, or Arbitrations. Though many times, in more then a month, there hath not been the least sale of any of the aforenamed Commodities, or occasion for any such sort of businesses.

And verily whom do you see sooner or later at the Exchange then these sort of people? And 'tis no wonder: for since they indeavour not to have the name of *brave Negotiants*, their principallest aim is to obtain the name of *great News-mongers*, and that hath so much tittle-tattle in it, that it requires a person free from all affairs and business to be imploied therein.

Here you may perceive them to be the most diligent of all others, oftner inquiring what tidings there are in the French, English, and Flanders

Letters; then to know what news from the Seas, concerning the arrivall or loss of Ships, or what Merchandizes, Commodities and Wares, are risen or fallen in price.

Nevertheless these make the greatest bawling and scolding at their Wives, if they have not their Dinners made ready for them precisely an hour before Change-time, just as if the main weight of all the Traffick and Negotiation at Change, lay upon their shoulders; though it only tends to follow the train, and to hear some news, or to seek some Pot-Companions.

These Blades will be sure also, in the Winter time by four, and in the Summer time by six a clock in the evening, to be precisely at the Coffe-houses; where, under the taking of a pipe of pure Spanish Tobacco, some dishes of Coffe, Chocolate, Sherbate, or Limonado, there is a relation made of the newest tidings, or what is most remarkable of things that have hapned here or there. They hear there no clock strike, nor think upon Wives, Children, or Servants, though it were never so late.

There's another sort of Men, that do not frequent the Exchange, and go out only about their Shop affairs, these we see taking their pleasures for several hours together at Queenhithe and other places, with selling of chatwood; and when they are a weary with walking and talking, away they go to the Plume of Feathers to rest themselves, and call for half a pint, or a pint of Sack, and some to the Strong Water Shop, and drink a quartern of Cinamon water, Clove-water, or Aqua mirabilis.

And these imagine themselves to be of the most orderly sort; by reason that some men, in the Summer time, take their pleasure most part of the morning, to be busie at their Wormwood Wine; and consume their afternoon in clashing and quafing off the bottels of Old Hock and Spaw-water. And when it grows cold, and the daies short, then they are early at the Strong-water Shop; and in the evening late in the Coffe-houses; and again twice or thrice a week precisely, and that more devouter then once in a Church, they are most certain to be found at the Playhouses.

Whilest others again are earnestly imploied in taking their pleasures in a Coach, or on horseback, ambling, trotting and gallopping along the high ways, from one Country Fair, or Horsemarket to another; and at every place where they see but a conveniency to stable their Horses, there they are certain to bait; and consume an infinite deal of time; especially if they happen to find any Horse-Coursers there to be chatting and chaffering with.

These are much like unto those that take delight in Pleasure-boats and Barges, who with the smallest gale of wind, are stormed out of all their occupations; nay, although they were never so important, yet the very breathing of a warm Zephyr blows not only all business out of their heads, but themselves in person out of their Shops and Counting-houses.

Here you may behold them with unwearied bodies rigging of their Masts, spreading of their Sails, hailing up their Spreet and Leeboards, and all in a sweat catching hold of the Oars to be rowing, whilst at home they are too weak or lazy to move or stir the least thing in the World, nay can hardly bring pen to paper. For to neglect such a gallant and pleasant day of weather, would be a crime unpardonable.

> *No lover of a boat, may stay within a Port,*
> *Though Shop and Office both, should dearly suffer for't.*

Others again are sworn Pigeon Merchants, and every Market day in the forenoon precisely, let it cost what it will, must be attending there, and the rest of the week both morning and afternoon at their Pigeon-traps. Here in they take an infinite pleasure, hushing up their Pigeons to flight, then observing the course they take; looking upon the turning of their Tumblers; and then to the very utmost, commending the actions, carriages and colours of their Great Runts, Small Runts, Carriers, Light Horsemen, Barberies, Croppers, Broad-tail'd Shakers, and Jacopins; taking care and making so much provision for their young ones, that they let both their own young, and the house-keeping, run to destruction.

But there are the Cock-Merchants surpass these abundantly; who, upon certain penalties, must at the least, thrice a week appear in the Cock-pit; and there, before the Battel begins, consume two or three hours at Tables, and in Wine, Beer and Tobacco; whilst they attend there the coming of their Adversaries and other lovers of the sport. Here then a view must be taken of each others Cocks, which are forsooth according to their merits and value, set apart in their Coops either in the yard, or above in the Garret, to be fed as is most convenient; and there's then a discourse held concerning them, as if they were persons of some extraordinary state, quality, and great valour.

Not a word must be spoke, (as much as if there were a penalty imposed upon it) but of Cock-fighting. Here Master Capon vaunts that his Game-Cock was hard enough for the gallant Shake-bag of Sir John Boaster; although Sir John Boasters famous Shake-bag, but three weeks before, had fought against that incomparable Game-Cock of Squire Owls-eg, and claw'd him off severely.

Here you may see abundance of Country Gentlemen and rich Farmers, coming from several parts with their Cocks in their bags to the Battel; hanging them up there in ample form till it be their turns to fight. And there also you may behold Lord Spendall brought thither in his Coach very magnificently, and carried home in no less state; but seldom goes away before he hath either won or lost a pretty number of Guinneys.

Yea there's Squire Clearpurse, with his Princely companion, who keep alwaies six and thirty Game-Cocks at nurse by the Master of the Pit; never goes away from thence, before he hath got, by his ordinary dunghill Cock that runs about the streets, and without false spurs too, half a score Crown-pieces, and as much more as will pay his reckoning in his pocket. But if they both begin to appear with their Shake-bags, then it is, Stand clear Gentlemen, here comes the honour of the Pit; and then the Master of the Pit must have out of each Battel for Sharpning the Spurs, and clipping of the neck feathers, half a Ginny; and then when the Battels ended, he brings into the reckoning half a Crown *extra* for Brandy, Salve, and cherishing and chafing it by the fire, &c. But for this, they have the honour also to be in the Chamber with the principallest Gentlemen, to sit in the best places of the Pit; to turn the hour-glass and like prudent Aldermen, in the presence of all the Auditors, to give their judgements touching the contending parties; where there are generally more Consultations, Advices, and Sentences, held and pronounced, then are to be found or heard of in the principallest Law-books or Statutes of the Kingdom.

It would be here an everlasting shame; if the Conqueror, like a Niggard, should carry all this money home; therefore the greatest part must be given and generously spent with the company. This is the duty of every one, whose Cock hath beaten anothers out of the Pit, and went away Crowing like a Conqueror. Nay, what's matter if it were all spent, its no such great peece of business; the honours more worth then the mony.

In the mean while it grows late in the night, and the good woman, with the Table covered, sits longing, telling every minute, and hoping for the coming home of him, who seems to find and take more pleasure in Cockfighling, then like a brave Game-Cock himself to enter into the Pit with his Wife. O most contrary and miserable Pleasure of marriage on the mens side.

But amongst these Cock-Merchants, I am of opinion, there's none hath more pleasure then the Master of the Pit; because he gets more for the feeding, clipping, salving, and anointing of them, &c. then ten good Nurses, and put them all together. And moreover he hath all the pleasure for nothing, and is mighty observant to feed and tickle their fancies, and obey their commands, that their delight therein may the more and more increase, and the reckoning also be ne'r a whit the less.

And these Lovers and Gentlemen are no sooner departed, but he laies him down very orderly in a very fashionable Bedstead, hung round about the Curtains and Vallians with Hens-Eg-shels suck'd out. But if he did, for the same purpose, suck out all the Cocks-Egshels, it would be a much more rare and pleasant sight.

There is yet another sort of men, which we in like manner find, that consume their time, neglect their occasion, and spend their mony with Dog-fighting, Bull and Bear-baiting, as the Cock-Merchants do with Cock-fighting. One way that they take pleasure in, is to bring their Dogs together, and there fight them for a Wager of five, or ten pound, and somtimes more; which mony must be set or stak'd down, though they hardly know how to find as much more again in the whole World, and there the poor Dogs by biting and tearing one anothers skins and flesh in pieces, for the pleasure of their fantastical Masters; and if the Wager be, in the least manner to be contradicted, then too't they go themselves, and thump and knock one another till they look more like beasts then men.

This being done, the next meeting is, to try their Bear and Bull-Dogs at the Bear Garden; the match being made, all their wits must be screw'd up to the highest, how to get mony to make good their wagers; though Wife, House and Family should sink in the mean while: Then away they go with their Tousers and Rousers to the Bear-garden, and then the Bull being first brought to the stake, the Challenger lets fly at her, and the Bull perceiving the Dog coming, slants him under the belly with her horns, and tosses him as high as the Gallerys, this is much laught at; but his Master, very earnestly and tenderly, catching him in the fall, tries him the second time, when he comes off with little better success: Then his Adversary lets loose his Dog at the Bull, who running close with his belly to the ground, fastens under the Bulls nose by the skin of the under-lip; the Bull shaking and roaring to get him loose, but he holds faster and faster; then up flie caps and hats, shouting out the excessive joy that there is for this most noble victory.

Now comes the Bear dogs, being stout swinging Mastives; and the Bearard having brought the Bear to the Stake, unrings him, and turns him about, so that he may see the Dog, that's to play at him; the Challenger lets fly his Dog, which being a cruel strong Cur rises up to the Bears nose, fastens and turns him topsy-turvy; there's no small joy and an eccho of Shouts that makes the very earth tremble; then there's pulling and hawling to get him off from the Bear: Then the Adversary let's fly his Dog, who coming to fasten, the Bear being furious and angry that he was so plagu'd with the first Dog, claps his paw about the back of him, and squeezes him that he howls and runs; there stands the Master, looking like an Owl in an Ivybush, to see the stakes drawn, and he haply with never a penny in his pocket, hath no mony at home, nor knows not where to get any. And that which vexeth him worst of all, is, that his delicate Dog is utterly spoil'd.

But we'l leave of these inhuman, and brutal stories; and rather relate the Confession of another sort of Men; who are generally of a longing temper, not much unlike to the big-bellied weak women; nay, sometimes do therein far surpas the Women: And altho they know that it is never so damagable or hurtfull unto them, yet dare boldly say:

> *When Women long, it harms by chance,*
> *But mens desire's a worser dance.*

And in this they are both bold and shameless, clear contrary to Women-kind; in so much that they without fear or terror, dare, at noon day, say to their Pot-companions: I have a mighty mind to a pipe of Tabacco, come lets go to the Sun, half Moon, or to the Golden Fleece, and smoke a pipe: where they rip up such a multiplicity of discourse, and consume so much time and Tabacco; that if they tasted neither beer nor wine, they might with all reason be upbraided to be debauch'd persons. But it would be a work as inexpressible as infinite to relate their longing appetites at all other times, to Musmillions, Seldry, Anchovis, Olives, or slubbring Caviart, with all their appurtenances. Much more their liquorishness at Oisters, where they stand greedily swallowing them up in the open shops, not giving themselves time to send for them to a Tavern, and eat them decently.

If they did thus, in the presence of their Wives, they might have some pleasure of it also: But the content hereof seems to consist therein, that either alone, or with their Fraternity, they may thus lustily satisfie their longing appetites.

Here we shall commend the Lovers of Tee, because they are willing to make use of it in the company of women; although there be now a daies so much formality used with it, and so much time idly spent in the consumption of it, that it seems almost as if this herb were found out, or brought over to no other purpose, then to be the occasion of an honest chatting-school, between men and women; where you may have intelligence of all that passes betwixt married and unmarried persons throughout the whole City. And wo be to them that have the least symptom of a meazle upon their tongue, for the true lovers of Tee, are like unto the Suppers up of Coffy, and are the best News-Mongers for all things that happens in the City, yea almost in all Kingdoms; and when you hear the men speak seriously of such matters; it is as if they had the best correspondence for intelligence out of all Princes Courts; but especially, if this miracle be wrought thereby, that the Water be changed in to Wine.

Others, who love neither Tee nor Coffy, and yet are very desirous to know what passes in the World; you may find mighty earnestly, for some hours, stand prating in the Booksellers Shops; alwaies asking what news is there, what Pamphlets, what Pasquils, what Plays, what Libels, or any of the like rubbish, is lately come out; and then they must buy and read them, let it cost what it will.

Here they make the sole balance of State-business. Here, with great prudence, discourse is held of the importantest State-affairs, and of the supreamest persons in authority; and in their own imaginations know more then both the Houses of Lords and Commons. Although they never sate in

Councel with any of their Footmen. Nay they know to the weight of an ace, and can give a perfect demonstration of it, which of the three Governments is best, Monarchy, Anarchy, or Democracy. Which many times takes such a deep root and impression upon them, and touches them so to the very heart, that they absolutely forget the governing of their needfull affairs which they went out about; for when they come to the place where their occasions lay; they find the person either long before gone abroad, or so imploied with his own business, that he can hardly a quarter do that he ought to do.

'Tis true some soft natured women, that are as innocent as Doves, observe not these sort of actions and tricks; but suffer themselves easily to be fopt off by their husbands; or else by a gentle salutation are appeased; but others who are cunninger in the cares of their Shops and Families, can no waies take a view of these doings with eys of pleasure.

Yet this is nothing near the worst sort, and is naught else but a kind of a scabbiness that the most accomplishedst marriages are infected with. And verily if the husbands do thus neglect their times, and their Wives, in the meanwhile, like carefull Bees, are diligent in looking after their Shop and housekeeping; they ought, when they do come home to speak their minds somthing freely to them.

But the imaginary authority of men, many times surges to such height, that it seems to them insupportable, to hear any thing of a womans contradiction, thinking, that all what ever they do, is absolutely perfect and uncontrolable. And can, on the contrary, when their Wives go to the Shambles or Market, reckon to a minute in what time they ought to be back again: And wo be to them, if they do, according to the nature of women, stand and prattle here or there their time away, concerning Laces, Cookery, and other houshold occasions.

But you, O wel married Couple, how pleasant it is to see that you two agree so well together! That either is alike diligent and earnest in taking care of their charge. That your husband many times saith unto you his houswife, my Dear, it is a curious fair day, go walk abroad, and give a visit to some or other of your good acquaintance; I shall tarry at home the whole day, and will take sufficient care of all things, and in the evening come and fetch you home, &c. And you again in like manner, upon a good occasion, releeve your husband, and take delight in his walking abroad with some good friends to take his pleasure, and to recreate and refresh his tired sences.

If he be a little sickish of that distemper and that he will somtimes spend a penny upon a Libel or new Tiding; that is a great pleasure for you, because you know that the Booksellers and Printers must live; and every fool must have one or t'other bawble to play with.

You had great reason to be dissatisfied if he consumed his mony in the Tavern or with Tables. But you know that Ben Johnsons Poems, and Pembrooks Arcadia, did so inchant you, that they forc't the mony out of your Pocket; yet they serv'd you in your Maiden estate with very good instructions, and shewing you many Vertues. You may therefore think, that such men who desire to surge higher in knowledge, will have somthing also to be reading. And it is most certain, whilest they are busie with that, their Wives are free from being controled. 'Tis also undeniable, that men cannot alwaies be alike earnest in their affairs; for verily if they be so, they are for the most part great *Peep in the Pots* and directers of their Wives, who have certainly their imperfections. And it is the principallest satisfaction, and greatest pleasure in marriage, when a woman winks or passes by the actions of her husband; and the husband in like manner the actions of his wife; for if that were not so, how should they now and then in passing by, throw a love-kiss at one another; or how should they at night be so earnest in pressing one another to go first to bed.

'Tis therefore, above all things, very needfull for the increasing of love, that a woman wink at many of her husbands actions; especially if he keep no correspondence with Tiplers, that will be alwaies in the Alehouses; and there too will be serv'd and waited upon, forsooth, to a hairs breadth; nay, and as we perceive, if the Wife brings in the Anchovis upon the Table, without watring them a little, as oftimes happens there, then the house is full of Hell and damnation. For these smaller sort of Gentlemen, are they who sow strife and sedition between man and wife, and continually talk of new Taverns and Alehouses, clean Pots, and the best Wine; they alwaies know where there is an Oxhead newly broach'd: and the first word they speak, as soon as they come together, is, Well Sir, where were you yesternight, that we saw you not at our ordinary meeting place? Ho, saies the t'other, 'twas at the *Blew Boar*, where I drunk the delicatest Wine that ever my lips tasted. You never tasted the like on't. If I should live a thousand year, the tast would never be out of my thoughts. Nay, if the Gods do yet drink Nectar, it is certainly prest out of those Grapes. Words cannot possibly Decipher or express the tast, though *Tully* himself, the father of eloquence, having drunk of it, would make the Oration. What do you think then, if you and I went thither immediately and drunk one pint of it standing? I am sure, Sir, that you will, as well as I, admire it above all others. Done it is, and away they go: But it is not long before you see those roses blossoming in their hands, of whose smell, tast, and colour a neat draught is taken, and an excellent exposition of the qualities. Yet the t'other Gentleman commends it to the highest; though he is assured that he tasted a Glass in Master *Empty Vessels* Cellar that was far delicater, and that he would far esteem beyond this. Nevertheless he acknowledges this to be very good. But the pint being out, the first word is, *Hangt, What goes upon one leg? Draws t'other pint of the same Wine.* And then they begin to find that the longer they drink, the better it tasts; which is an undeniable sign that it is pure good Wine. And this pint being out again; presently saies the t'other, *All good things consist in three:* so that we must have the t'other pint. Where upon the second saith, As soon as this is out, we will go with the relish of it in our mouths to Master Clean Pints, to tast his and this against each other. I am contented, so said so done; and thus by the oftentimes tasting and retasting, they grow so mighty loving, that it is impossible for them to depart from one another, because they every foot say, they cannot part with an empty Pot, and this love in a few hours grows on so hot, that the love of the Wife is totally squencht; not only drawing men mightily out of their business, but keeping them late out from their families; and making them like incarnate Divels against their Wives. From whence proceeds, that when they come either whole or half drunk home, there is nothing well to their minds, but they will find one thing or another to controul, bawl or chide with.

To these also may be adjoined those who generally resort to the Miter, Kings Arms, and Plume of Feathers, or some other places where they commonly make their bargains for buying and selling of Goods and Merchandizes; from whence they seldom come before they have spent a large reckoning, and lost more then three of their five sences; thinking themselves no less rich then they are wise; and ly then very subtlely upon the catch to overreach another in a good and advantagious bargain; by which means they themselves are somtimes catcht by the nose with a mouldly old sort of unknown commodity, that they may walk home with, by weeping cross; and next morning there they stand and look as if they had suckt their Dam through a hurdle, and know not which way to turn themselves with their Merchandize they have made; in this manner, bringing their Wives and Children (if they let them know it) into excessive inconveniences; and for all this want for nothing of grumbling and mumbling.

> *Some sorts of men,*
> *Are Tyrants when,*
> *Their thirsty Souls are fill'd:*
> *They scold sore hot*
> *Like* Peep in th' Pot
> *And never can be still'd.*
> *They talk and prate*
> *At such a rate,*
> *And think of nought but evil;*
> *They fight and brawl,*
> *And Wives do mawl,*
> *Though all run for the Divel.*
> *But at their draugh,*
> *They quaff and laugh*
> *Amongst their fellow creatures.*
> *They swear and tear*
> *And never fear*
> *Old* Nick *in his worst features.*
> *Who would but say*
> *Then, by the way*
> *That Woman is distressed,*
> *Who must indure*
> *An Epicure*
> *With whom she'll ne'r be blessed.*

In this last many Fathers commit great errors, who, when they are hot-headed with multiplicity of Wine, take little regard of the bad examples they shew unto their Children and Families. Nay some there are that will in their sobrest sence go with their sons, as if they were their companions, into a Tavern without making any sort of difference; and also, when there is a necessity or occasion for it, know but very slenderly how to demonstrate their paternal prudence and respect; but in this manner let loose the bridle of government over their children.

Thus I knew an understanding Father do, who with some other Gentlemen, and his son, being upon a journy together, to take care of some important affairs; but seeing that at every Inn where they came, that his fellow-travellers were resolute blades, and that he must pay as deep to his son as himself; exhorted his son to take his full share of all things, and especially of the Wine; every foot whispering him in the ear, Peter, drink, and then after a little while, again, Peter, drink; And as he recommended this so earnestly to his son, he himself very diligently lost no time to get his share; which continued so long that going out of the chamber for their necessities, they both fell into a channel, where clasping each other in the arms, the son said, Father! are we not now like brothers?

By this we may observe, what the Father of a Family, by his examples, may do. But you, O well-match'd Woman, have no need to fear this sort of president in your husband, because he is a perfect hater of excessive drinking, and an enemy to such company that alwaies frequent Taverns and Ale-houses; and if he doth go once among good acquaintance, and take a glass more then ordinary, which is but seldom, there's nothing that he doth less then maunder and mumble; but he's all for kissing, hugging and dallying; hating pot-company to the highest, or those that make it their business, or spend their times in the Summer with going a Fishing, and in the Winter go a Birding; upon which sort of Gentlemen this old rime was made:

> *Who in the Winter Bird, and Summers go a Fishing,*
> *Have no bad meat in Tub, that is not worth the dishing.*

But your husband on the contrary, takes especial care of his affairs; and for the pleasure and ease of his wife, goes himself to market, there buies a good joint of meat or a Fowl, and gets it made ready, and sits down and eats it with his beloved: Then when he and you have very relishingly satisfied your appetites, and drunk two or three glas of wine into the bargain, he invites you very quietly to walk up stairs into your chamber to say a day-lesson. Well who could wish for greater Pleasure then this!

O good Woman, how happy are you, if, as well as your husband you can keep your self in these joys and delights. What state or condition is there in this World that may be compared to such a loving, friendly and well accomplished match! For without jesting, it happens hardly once in a thousand times that a match falls out so well. And although it did, yet it is not free from a thousand crosses and dissatisfactions, which are done unto you either by children, wicked friends, or somtimes bad neighbours: and are oftentimes so many, that if they were all drawn up in one Picture; we should, in good truth, see more grief and horror in it, then is demonstrated in the very Picture of Hell it self. But one pound of the hony of sweet love, can easily balance a hundred weight of that terrible and bitter Wormwood.

But where is there one among all the whole number of tender young Gentlewomen, who being incountred by an airy exquisite Lover, that doth not start back with a thousand troublesom cogitations; and beleeves, that he, who thus earnestly affects her, is at the least possessed with one of these terribly evil natures? Nay, perhaps with some what else, as a cross-grain'd pate, a grumbling gizzard, not wel in his sences, jealous thoughts, or the actions of a Cotquean are his companions; and that is more then all these, keeps hid a certain imbecility in his defective nature; which is no waies to be discovered till the nuptial rites be absolutely celebrated.

This seems to be a great occasion and reason to have an abhorrance for marrying. But when we begin again with serious judgement to consider, the weaknesses, strange humors, and deficiences, that the most gaudiest and neatest Ladies are subject to; experience will teach us, that they are Cakes bak'd of one Dough, and Fruits of one Tree.

And therefore they are very happy, if two of one mind, and alike natured meet together; but if two of contrary humors happen together, there is nothing to be expected but grief, sorrow, and destruction; unless it happen that the understanding of the one knows extraordinarily how to assist the weakness of the other; by somtimes letting loose a rope and then drawing it in again; whereby they may the prudentlier sail against wind and tide. These do arrive in the Haven of the Pleasures of Marriage, whereas others on the contrary suffer most miserable Shipwrack.

The Sixth Pleasure.

The Woman hath got the Breeches. What mischeefes arise by it. Counsel for the unmarried. To shun those that are evil natured.

Under a thousand Pleasures that we find in the estate of marriage, it is none of the least, to see the Woman put the breeches on, seeming that she will act the part of a Jack-pudding. But melancoly men oftentimes cannot bear with such sort of jesting, and presently bawl and rail at such a Woman, calling her a Monster, or some other ill name. Although they know very well that such sort of Monsters are now a daies so common, that if they were all to be shewn in Booths for farthings a peece, there would be less spectators, then there was to see the Sheep with five legs, or the great Crocodile.

Verily, such men are unhappy, and they do not a little also neglect these Pleasures; when they, forsooth, think that by the putting on of the breeches, must be understood that they are over Lorded, and that the Hen crows louder then the Cock. O miserable man, if your head be possest with this kind of frenzy, and can't be removed! Verily, if you had but seen the Plate of the Women fighting for the Breeches, you would be of another judgement. For in those daies the man was glad to be rid of them, if he could but get the lining untorn or indamaged; for he saw perfectly that the World was at that time so full of those pretty Beldams, that there was begun a most bloody War between the better sort of Gentlewomen, and the meaner degree of Women, for the gaining of the Breeches, wherein Ketels and Pans, Tongs and Fireshovels, Spinning-wheels, Brooms and Maps were all beaten out of fashion. And it may very well be thought, that if the Woman had put them on at first, and so have helpt him to have kept them, this wonderfull and destructive War would never have risen to that fury. Therefore it is no small prudence of the Women in these daies, who are descended from that family, to take care, at the very first, for the good of their husbands, that the Breeches may be well preserved.

But let's be serious, and pass by all these kind of waggeries; if we consider the husband as Captain, and the Wife as Lieutenant, is it not in the highest degree necessary, that she should have also a part of the masculine knowledge and authority? Besides, women must be silent in Politick and Church-government, why should not they have somthing to say in those places where they are houswives? We see certainly, that the men, for the most part, cannot tarry at home, and will be going hither or thither to take the air, or for his pleasure, or to smoke a pipe of Tabacco; as is shew'd you in the Fifth Confession; if then, in the mean while, the Woman, through occasion of some Customers in the Shop, or in the government of the Men and Maid-servants should not in some measure shew that she had in part the Breeches on, and that she could in the absence of her Captain, take care of his Command; how is it possible that the Trading should be kept in order, and the Children and Servants well governed? I will not so much as mention that there are several men, who are so dull-brain'd, and so excessive careless, that if they had not had the good fortunes to get notable sharp-witted young women to their Wives; they of themselves would have been quickly out of breath, and might now perhaps be found in the Barbado's or Bermoodo's planting Tabacco.

O stout Amazonians, who thus couragiously, take the Weapons in hand, to defend and protect your Husbands, Children, Servants and houskeeping; why should not you have as great commendations given you, as those noble Souls of your Sex had in former times? and who would not rather ingage in the imbracing of you, then any waies to affront or bespatter you?

I know wel enough there will come some times a whiffling blade, that will be relating one or other long-nosed story, how like a drunken Nabal, he was well instructed by his prudent and diligent wife; and how little that he would obey or listen to the commands of so brave a Captain; but they will very seldom or never say any thing what grounds or provocatives they have given her for so doing.

Nevertheless my intent is, not so much to flatter the evil or bad natured women, as if their throwing out their ire upon their husbands, had alwaies a Lawfull excuse or cause. Just as Xantippe did, who was Socrates's wife, think that she had reason enough on her side to scold, brawl at, and abuse that wise and good natured Philosopher, and to dash him in the face with a whole stream of her hot Marish piss. Or that it did any waies become that hot-ars'd whorish Faustina, to govern that sage and understanding Emperor

Marcus Aurelius. By no means, for then that hot-spirited, and high minded sex would prick up their Peacocks-tails so much the higher. But happy would all these hair-brain'd houswives be, if they had such Tutors to their husbands, as Aurelius was; 'tis most certain, that then that corrupt seed, would be cropt in the very bud and not be suffered to come to perfection.

Yet you new married Couple, are both in heart and mind concordant, and all your delight is to please each others fancy: you have no difference about the Supremacy; for the Authority of the one is alwaies submitted to the other; and so much the more because your husband never commands you as if you were a Maid; but with the sweetest and kindest expressions, saith, my Dearest, will you bid the Maid draw a glass of Beer or Wine, or do this or that, &c. Oh if you could but both keep your selves in this state and posture, how happily and exemplarily would you live in this World! But it happens many times, that the Women through length of time, do take upon them, and grow to be so free, that they will be solely and totally Master; and if their husbands through kind-heartedness have given them a little more then ordinary liberty, they will have the last word in spight of fate.

So have I seen one who could by no means keep her self in that first and Paradice-like life; who observing her husbands good nature, thought her self wise enough to govern all things, and to bring him to her Bow; which, by degrees, to his great discontent, did more and more increase in matters of the housekeeping.

But it hapned once that the good man, went to the Market, and having bought a delicate Capon, meets with a friend, whom he invited to be his guest; and going home with it, his wife powts, maunders and mutters and looks so sowr that the guest saw well enough how welcome he should be. The good man with fair and kind words sought to remove this, which was in some measure done.

But a pretty while after, the goodman being in the market, buies a couple of delicate Pullets, and sends them home with a Porter; but the Wife told him she had made ready somthing else, and had no need of them; therefore, let him say what he would, made him bring them back again: The good man meeting with the Porter, and perceiving the cross-grainedness of his wife, sends them to a Tavern to be made ready, and gets a friend or two along with him to dispatch them, and dript them very gallantly with the juice of Grapes. At this, when he came home, his wife grin'd, scolded, and bawl'd; yet done it was, and must serve her for a future example. And she on the contrary persisting in her stif-necked ill nature, made a path-road for the ruine of her self and family, because he afterwards, to shun his wife, frequented more then too much Taverns and Alehouses, and gave the breeches solely to his wife.

Not long ago, just in the like manner, there married an indifferent handsom Gentlewoman, with a proper, handsom, honest and good natured Gentleman; but the Gentlewoman imagining her self to be as wise as a Doctor, acted the part of a Domineerer, controuling, grumbling and chiding at all whatsoever he did; insomuch that all his sweet expressions could no waies allay her; but rather augmented her rage; yea insomuch that at last she saluted him with boxes and buffettings. But he seeing that no, reasons or perswasions would take place, and that she grew the longer the more furious, locks the dore to, and catches her by the coif, instructing her with such a feeling sence, that at last she got open a window and leaps out, thereby escaping the remaining part of that dance. Away she flies immediately to her Father and her Brother, but they, very well knowing her ill-natured obstinacy, both denied her houseroom. Yet the next day, through the intercession of others, there was a pacification made and a truce concluded on, which did not long continue so. For she, beginning again her former wicked actions, made him run to the Tavern there to allay his disturbed sences, leaving her to wear the Breeches. But now they are rid of mony, credit, respect, and every thing else.

Another Gentlewoman of late daies, seeing that she had married a good mild-natured husband, that was not guilty of any vice, exercised her authority and wickedness so much the more over him; yea so far, that in the presence of several neighbors she oftentimes knockt, thumpt, and cudgelled him; that at last she was called by every one *The incarnate Divel.* But he, after some years of suffering this martyrdom, hapning to dy, there comes another Lover very suddenly to cast himself away upon this Hellish peece of flesh; but she had of him, being a just punishment, such a beloved, that he thunderd her three times as bad about, as she did her first husband; and then flew Pots, Kans and Glasses ringling and gingling along the flore, and she on the top of them, well and warm covered with good thumps and fistycuffs, and somtimes traild over the flore by the hair of the head. O miserable terrors of such a horrible State and condition! Who can but shake and quiver, yea with fear start back, when they begin to feel the least motion to the same in their bodies? and so much the more, because that we see that this present World is so mightily replenished with such numbers of monstrous, wicked and unhappy women, who hide their wickedness and ill natures under their powdered locks, and flattring looks; and like a Camelion, in their Maiden estate, will be agreeable to all things that are propounded to them; but being married, they abandon all rationality, make their own passions their masters, and cannot understand by any means the pleasures of their husbands. Though they certainly know, and have daily experience, that there is nothing under the Sun, which hath a bewitchinger power upon the hearts of their husbands, then the friendliness and kind compliance of their Wives. This hath in ancient times done a thousand wonders and is as yet the most powerfull to drive all stuborn and ill-natured humors out of the heads of men; and can lead them, as it were by the hand, in to the paths of Reason, Equity and Love.

O happy Women, who, in this manner have the hearts of men in your hands, and can bring the same to your obedience where you will; what means and waies ought you not to indeavour by dallyings and kind actions to gain the same on your side! you certainly know, that the main Butt which is aim'd at by all mankind, is to pass through this short life of ours with pleasure and quietness: But alas! what life, what rest, what pleasure can he possess in this World, who hath hapned upon a scolding, and no waies friendly wife?

Oh if all Lovers knew this so well, they would never suffer themselves to be led away captive by the jettish eys, and marble-like breasts, or strangle themselves in the curled locks of women; but would imbrace their kind naturedness to be the surpassingest beauty.

But the carnal desires, and covetousness of mony, blindeth the eys of so many, that oftentimes for the satisfaction thereof, they will, contrary to all exhortations, run headlong, and cast themselves into a pit of infinite horrors and vexations of Spirit: chusing rather a proud, finical, blockheaded Virgin with two thousand pound, then a mean, kind-hearted, understanding one, with ten thousand Vertues.

This was that which the prudent King Lycurgus sought to prevent, when he gave out his commands that no Parents should give any portions with their Daughters in marriage, or might leave them any thing for an inheritance; because he would not have them to be desired in marriage by any, but for their beauty and vertues; in those daies the vitious remained, just as now doth the poor ones, most of them unmarried, and cast aside, and every Maid was hereby spur'd up, that her Vertues might in brightness and splendor surpass others.

Happy are you, O Father of the Family, who without the least thoughts of Lycurgus, have made so good a choice and have gotten a Wife that is beautifull, rich, good natured, and vertuous; you learnt first to know her well, that you might the better woe her, and so be happy in marriage. Make this your example, O all you foolish and wandring Lovers, who are so desirous to tast of the Pleasures and sweetness of marriage; and are somtimes so disquieted and troubled till you cast your selves upon an insulting, domineering Wife, who perhaps hath the Breeches already on, and will vex you with all the torments imaginable in the World. Do but use these few remedies for your squandered brains, and be assured they will bring you to have good fortune and tranquility.

Search not after great Riches, but for one of your own degree; for the Rich are insulting, self-conceited, and proud.

Admire no outward beauty; because they are proud of their beauty, and imagine themselves to be Goddesses, whom their husbands ought to obey.

Shun those who are much lesser then your self: For when a mean one finds her self promoted by a great Match, she is much prouder and self-conceited then one of a good extraction; and will much sooner than another indeavour to domineer over her husband.

Dissemble not in your wooing. For dissimulation deceives its own Master.

Be not too hasty. For a thing of importance must be long and prudently considered of, before a final conclusion can be made.

Follow the advice of understanding friends. For to be wise, and in love, was not given to the Gods themselves.

Chuse no Country wench: For she'l want a whole years learning, before she'l know how to shine upon a house or Office, and two years to learn to make a cursie.

If you marry, arm your self with patience. For he that hath the yoke of marriage upon his shoulders, must patiently suffer and indure all the disquiets and troubles that that estate is subject to.

If these things be observed by you innocent and wandring Lovers, they will much assist you in your choice, but not preserve you from being a slave; because the Gentlewoman whom you have chosen, hath till this time be past, had one or other ill condition, which she knew how to hide and dissemble with, that you never so much as thought of, or expected from her. Cornelius Agrippa knew this in his daies, when he said, men must have and keep their wives, e'en as it chanceth; if they be (saies he) merry humored, if they be foolish, if they be unmannerly, if they be proud, if they be sluttish, if they be ugly, if they be dishonest, or whatsoever vice she is guilty of, that will be perceived after the wedding, but never amended. Be therefore very vigilant, you wandring Lovers, and sell not your liberty at so low a price, which cannot be redeemed again with a whole Sea of repentances.

And you, O silent Gentlewomen, methinks you long to know whether there be no remedies for you to be had, that you may also be as well arm'd against the rigid natured, subtle and dissembling Lovers, as well as they have against the vitious Gentlewomen; take notice, that since you have subjected your selves to that foolish fashion of these times, never of your selves to go a wooing; but with patience will expect who will come for you, that rule must be first observed, and regard taken of him that cometh, then it is the time to consider, principally.

Whether he loveth you for your mony, or for your beauty.

Inquire whether he have a good method, or way, for the maintaining of a Family. For if he have not that to build upon, the whole foundation will tumble.

Search also whether he be of an honest, rather then great extraction. For Vertue is the greatest Gentility.

Inquire also whether he be a frequenter of Alehouses; especially of such as are of an evill reput.

> *To be a lover of such houses,*
> *Makes him to think of other Spouses.*

If he be covetous of honour, he hath several other Vertues.

Hate a Gamester like the Plague; for they are consumers of all; nay their very gain is loss.

Abhor a person of no imploy, or gadder along the streets; for they are fit for nothing.

If you marry, shew all honour, respect, and love to your husband. Indeavour not to Lordize over him; because that, both by Heaven and nature is given unto him.

In so doing, you will have, as well as our new-married Couple, the expectation of a happy match; which though it falls out well, yet is subject to severall accidental corruptions; as you will perceive in the further Confession of the insuing Pleasures, even as if they were a Looking-glass.

The Seventh Pleasure.

The bad times teaches the new married Couple. Makes them brave housekeepers. They take in Lodgers, and give good examples to their Children.

It was formerly very pleasant living, when Trading and Merchandizing flourished so nobly, that every evening people were fain to carry a whole drawer full of mony out of the Counter in to the Counting-house; and then the good woman had alwaies two or three hours work to sort it, before they could so much as think of going to bed: but it seems that destructive War, as being a scourge from Heaven, for our dissatisfied Spirits; hath so lamentably humbled the Land of our Nativity, that there are very few who have not now just causes enough to complain.

And you, O young people, shall be witnesses hereof, who have already, in that short time that you have been married, experience that things do not alwaies run upon wheels so merrily as was expected. 'Tis true you possess the Pleasure of an indifferent Trade, as well as the rest of your Neighbours; but it is not in any measure to be compared with those golden daies that your Ancestors had, when they could lay up so much wealth, and yet complained they had but little custom.

Published by The Navarre Society, London.

Verily, when I rightly consider it, methinks you are happier then they were. For at that time all their delight was, by a covetous frugality, to reap much riches together, and though that hapned very well, yet there was never enough; for mony is no impediment to a covetous soul because it alwaies yearns for more. But now on the contrary, it is esteemed to be very nobly done, and people take an absolute delight in it, if they can but tell how to scrape so much together, that they may keep the Dunners from their dores, bring up their children indifferently well, and pay the taxations and impositions that are imposed upon them. In good truth, they that can do this now, are worthy of as much credit and reputation, as those were that prospered much in former daies; and their Pleasure ought not to be lesser then the others before was.

O happy Successors, who through the contentment of your minds, possess now as great Pleasure, as your rich Parents formerly did, in their plentifull daies. Verily, your gain is comparatively better then theirs, because you are satisfied with so much less; and by consequence when the hour of death approaches, you can so much the easier depart from this World, by reason you shall not leave so many knives behind you that may cut your childrens throats.

Therefore if your Trading should come to diminish more; and that you can hardly tell how to keep both ends together; then comfort your selves with this happiness; to the end that the Pleasures of your marriage, may thereby not be eclipsed. For in bad times you must as diligently search after the Pleasures of Marriage, as for gain and good Trading.

But it seems, as you imagine, that this Pleasure rather decreases then increases; because that the small trading, is accompanied with bad paiment; and where ever you run or go to dun, you find no body at home, but return back to your house with empty pockets. For there is Master Highmind, and Squire Spightfull, who come every day in their Velvet Coats to the Change, are not in the least ashamed that the Goods, which they bought to be paid ready down, after the expiration of a full year, are not yet paid. And Master Negligent, who is alwaies in an Alehouse, and seldom to be found in his Counting-house or at the Change, thinks it is abundance too early in July, so much as to look upon the reckoning of last New-year, much less to pay it.

Nevertheless others have their Creditors also, and this Bill of Exchange, and that Assignment must be paid at their due times; yea, and the Winter is approaching, Wood and Coals must be bought, the Cellar furnisht with Beer and Wine, and some Firkins of Butter, and provision made for the powdring-tub to be filled, as well as several other sorts of necessaries for the Family that will be wanting. Insomuch that this affords but a very slight appearance of concluding the year in Pleasure.

But, O carefull House Father, if you knew in what a happy age you live, you would not go away so dissatisfied, but imbrace all these affairs very joifully for extraordinary Pleasures.

Hitherto you have gone forward like one young and unexperienced, and have meant with Master Dolittle, alias John the Satisfied, that things were to be done with kissing, licking, dallying, and other fidle fadles; but now you are come to a more sober, serious understanding, and to have mans knowledge, and the same prudent conduct that your Parents and Friends had, when they were assembled together about your Contract of Marriage, and then thought of all these things. Now you are grown to be a Master of Arts in the University of Wedlock. And great Juno laught, that Venus hath so long hoodwink'd you.

Come on then, these films being now fallen, from your eys, do but observe how prudent carefull Time hath made you, and how circumspect and diligent you begin to be that you may get through the World with honour, commendations, and good respect; how like a care taking Father you are now providing for your Wife, Children, and whole Family. Oh if your Father and Mother were now alive, how would they rejoice in this your advancement; which are indeed the upright Pleasures of Marriage. For all married people, draw the cares, here mentioned, along with them; though they come with a bag full of mony about their necks in to the World.

Do but see, till now you have had a brave and splendant house, paid great rent, only for your self and family to live in; now you begin to consider with understanding and Pleasure, whether a dwelling of less price would not serve as well, in which you might have a Chamber or two that you could let out to some civil Gentlemen, who might diet with you; it would help to pay the rent, and bring some profit in besides; and it is all one trouble for boiling, roasting, and going to Market: the day goes about nevertheless, and the Maid suits her work accordingly. And moreover, you have good company of them in your house, and alwaies either one or another at dinner begins to relate some kind of pretty discourse, that is continually very pleasurable and delightfull to be heard.

Observe how glad your Wife is concerning this resolution! There hath not been these three years any Proclamation published, which pleased her fancy better: for now her husband will have some pastime, and good company at home, so that he needs not go to seek it in the evening in Alehouses or other places. Well who cannot but see here how one may learn through honest Time and Experience, what Pleasures they are accompanied with?

But stay a little, and to be serious with you, when you get such guests, you'l see how they will plague you; for the general imaginations of such Gentlemen are, that all the monies they spend, is pure gain, and that the Landlord and Landlady alwaies ought to provide such sort of diet as they have most a mind to: and though it be never so well drest, yet there shall hardly come one dish to the Table, but they will be finding fault that this hath too much pepper in it, and that too much salt, &c. Besides all this, both Maids and Men, and all what's in the house, must be at their commands; nay be readier and nimbler to serve them then their Master and Mistriss. And that's more, you are deprived of the whole freedom of your house and table. It happens also many times, that they have so many visiters, and runners after them, that they require more attendance; and the maid hath more work with them alone, then the whole house-keeping besides.

This is the general course of all fellow Commoners; I will not say any thing of a worser sort, which are many times amongst them; who run in the mornings to Strong-water Shops, and in the afternoon to Taverns; where they so disguise themselves, that one must be ashamed for honest people who are in the Shop, or standing upon the flore, that sees them either come in a dores or down from their Chambers, hardly able to stand; besides they value not if they tarry out late at nights; and, if it be possible, they will intice the good man of the house to debauch with them. And then again they are seldom free from private chatting and pratling with the Maid and Men servants.

But perhaps you may light of a better sort, which Time, who is the mother of all things, will make appear. Let it be as it will, here is alwaies pleasure and delight to be expected for the good man, because the good woman by this means increaseth to more knowledge of housholding affairs; and therefore is alwaies busie, like a prudent mother, in educating, governing, and instructing her children.

Yea, if you, O Father of the Family, will go a little further, and behold with clear eys, how far your wife, through these bad times, is advanced in understanding and knowledge; I do assure you, you will find your self as ravisht with joy; because this is as great a transformation as ever Ovid writ of. For whereas at the beginning of your marriage, all her cogitations were imploied for the buying of large Venetian Looking-glasses, Indean Chainy, Plush Stools and Chairs, Turkish Tapistry, rich Presses and Tables, yea and whatsoever else was needfull for neatness and gallantry; we see now, that all her sences are at work, where ever they may or can be, to save and spare all things, and to take care that there may not so much as a match negligently be thrown away.

Formerly, your good wife used, by reason of her youth, and want of knowledge, to walk very stately, hand in hand with you, along the streets, finically trickt up with powdered locks, and a laced Gorget and Gown, and had commonly need of, at the least, three hours time, before she, with the help of two serviceable assistants, could be put to her mind in her dress; and then again all her discourse was of walking or riding abroad, and of junketting and merriment; whereas now on the contrary, seeing the small gain, she is sparing of all things, and ordring it to the best advantage for the family; without so much as setting one foot out of her House or Counter unnecessarily. Never thinking more of gadding abroad, to take pleasure; but finds all her delight by being busie in her houskeeping, amongst her children and servants. Here you may behold her driving the maid forwards, and setting her a spinning, to keep the sleep out of her eys; and with this intent also that she may have the delight to get yarn enough ready towards Winter, to let a brave Web of Linnen be woven for the service of the Family. Yea, and here she shews you, that though before she was but a Bartholomew Baby, that she is now grown to be a brave houswife. And that, if need requires, she can put a hand to the plough stoutly.

O happy man, who in such a sad and troublesom time, can find out so many Pleasures of Marriage, and who art already so well instructed in that most illustrious School!

'Tis true, you will meet with some jeering prattle-arses, that will say, is this that brave couple, that there was such a noise made of when they were married! Is this the Gentlewoman that used to go so costly in her Gorgets and Gowns! Goes she now with a plain wastcoat! alas and welladay! doth her feathers begin to hang thus! Well, is this the Gentlewoman that used alwaies to keep two maids! Can she now make a shift with a little wench that earns her wages with spinning, and her diet with doing the house work? it must certainly ly very nastily and sluttishly at her house.

'Tis very true, this might happen to you, and it would seem to eclipse the Sun of your Pleasures of Marriage very much; if you had not now, O well matcht Couple, through the instruction of the winged Time, gotten such prudent eys that you can easily see through such vain and simple Clouds.

But now you apprehend, to your great joy and comfort, that this arrow comes out of the Quiver of such as are indebted to every body, and suffer themselves daily to be durrid; who are continually pratling with the Neighbors, and gadding along the streets; they take notice of every dore that opens, and neglect their own houskeeping having no understanding to govern it; the dishes, pots and pans are alwaies standing in the middle of the flore; and Benches and Stools are all covered and ly filled with the Childrens dirty clouts, and the Windows are so thick with dirt, that the Sun can hardly shine through them. Whose first word is, when any body comes into their house, What! by reason of these sad times a body hath neither joy nor delight in their houskeeping. If we wash the glass windows, they are in danger of breaking, and at present we cannot bear with any losses. And these ordinarily have more pratling and felling then any other women, and no body knows any thing better then these sworn tittletattlers; they are seldom to be found with a pin-cushion upon their laps; and are the occasion that their houses, children and Maids stink of filth and sluttishness, with their cloaths out at the elbous, and their stockins out at the heels. Whilest their husbands sit in the Alehouses, and seek by drinking, domineering and gaming to drive these damps of the sad times out of theire brains; which continueth so long, till that all is consumed, and they both fly damnably in debt to their Creditors.

Well then, you worthy and faithfull Houskeepers, you see now the unhappy state and condition of these venomous controulers of others: And on the contrary, you may perceive how happy the bad times, like a prudent Instructor, makes you; what a quantity of understanding and delight it imparts unto you; whilest you both, with joint resolution, diligent hands and vigilant eys, indeavor the maintenance and setting up of your Family. Be assured, that this care and frugality will so root it self in your very bones, that although the times changed and grew better, you would reserve a stedfast delight in the promoting the good and benefit of your houskeeping; and withall leave to your children such riches and good examples, that they will follow your footsteps of carefulness with delight, and lay a hand to the plough, thereby to demonstrate that they were of a good extraction: which if it so happen, you will inherit one of the greatest and desiredst Pleasures that is to be found in the Married estate.

The Eighth Pleasure.

The Parents would bring up their son in their way of Trade, but he hath no mind to't. He is put to School out of the City. Grows a Scholler, commits much mischief. Is apprehended and informed what a Schollerlike life is.

Uds life, now I thinke on't, amongst the Pleasures of Mariage, this is none of the least, when one sees their children feed well, and grow up healthfully and merrily; and their stomacks in a morning are as soon open as their eys; then at noons they can claw it away at a good dish, as well as persons of full growth and years; and about four of the clock their appetites are again prepared for an afternoons lunchion; insomuch that they can eat you into poverty, without making their teeth bleed. O it is such a delight to see that they continually grow up so slovenly and wastfully in their cloaths, that they must needs have every half year almost a new suit, and that alwaies a little bigger; whereby the Father sees that he shall in short time have a son to be his man in the shop, and the mother a daughter to be her caretakester and controulster of the Kitchin.

Thus we advance in the estate of Mariage, from one pleasure to another. O how happy you'l be, if your children be but pliable and courteous, and grow up in obedience, and according to your example! But we see in the generality, that as their understanding increases, that also their own wills and desires do in like manner not diminish.

Perhaps you meet with some such symptoms as these are in your own son; for having been some years learning the Latine Tongue at Pauls or Merchant Tailors School; he is then inveagled by some of the neighbors sons to go with them to learn the Italian or French language; to which purpose they know of a very delicate Boarding school a little way out of the City; and then they baptize it with the name, that he hath such a longing and earnest desire to learn it, that he cannot rest in the night for it.

What will you do? The charge there of, the bad times, and the necessity you have for him at home, makes you perswade him from it, and to proffer him convenient occasions in the City; but what helps it, the fear of drawing the child from that which he has so much a mind to; and may be, that also, wherein his whole good fortune consists, causes you to take a resolution to fullfill his desire. Away he's sent then, and agreed for. And then there must be a Trunk furnisht, with all manner of linnen and cloaths, with other toys and sweet meats, and mony in his pocket to boot.

Having been some small time there he sends some letters for what he wants. Which is, with recommendations of being saving and diligent, sent unto him. And it is no small pleasure for the Parents, if they do but see that he is an indifferent proficient. All their delight and pleasure is, when time will permit, to go to their son, and to shew him their great love and affection.

But the Daughter, which goes along with her Mother, is kindled with no small matter of jealousie to see that her Brother puts her Parents to so much charge, gets what he pleases, and that their minds are never at rest about him. When she, on the contrary, being at home, is thrust by her Mother into the drudgery of the house, or kept close to her needle. Yet these are pacified with a fine lace, a ring, or some such sort of trinkom trankoms; and then with telling them into the bargain, when your brother comes home he shall keep the shop.

This the Father is in expectation of. And the son being come home, gives a great Pleasure to his Father and Mother, by reason he speaks such good Latin and Italian, and is so gentile in his behaviour: but to look to the shop, he hath no mind to. Say what they will, talk is but talk. All his desire and mind is to go to the University either of Oxford or Cambridge. And although the Father in some measure herein yeelds and consents; the Mother, on the other side, can by no means resolve to it; for her main aim was, that her son should be brought up in the shop; because that in the absence, or by decease of her husband, he might then therein be helpfull to her. Besides that, it is yet fresh in her memory, that when her Brother studied at Oxford, what a divellish deal of mony it cost, and what complaints there come of his student-like manner of living. Insomuch that there was hardly a month past, but the Proctor of the Colledge, or the Magistracy of the City must have one or other penalty paid them.

Now they try to imploy the son in the shop, who delights in no less melody then the tune of that song: letting slip no occasion that he can meet with to get out of the shop; and shew himself, with all diligence, willing to be a Labourer in the Tennis Court, or at the Bilyard Table; and is not ashamed, if there be hasty work, in the evening, to tarry there till it be past eleven of the clock. What a pleasure this vigilance is to the Father and Mother, those that have experience know best. Especially when they in the morning call their son to confession, and between Anger and Love catechize him with severall natural and kind reproofs.

'Tis but labour lost, and ill whistling, if the horse won't drink. What remedy? turn it, and wind it so as you will.

> *The son his mind to study is full bent,*
> *Or else will live upon his yearly rent.*

Here must be a counsell held by wisdom, prudence, love and patience. Here also the imaginations of incapableness or want of monies must be conquered; for to constrain a son to that he hath no mind to, is the ready way to dull his genious, and perhaps bring him to what is worser, to wit, running after whores or Gaming. And to teach him how to live upon his yearly means, the tools are too damn'd costly. So that now the Parents have true experience of the old Proverb.

> *The Children in their youth, oft make their Parents smart,*
> *Being come to riper years, they vex their very heart.*

Nevertheless, after you have turn'd it and wound it so as you will, the sending of him to the University of Oxford bears the sway; and there to let him study Theology being the modestest Faculty, by one of the learnedst and famousest Doctors. And verily, he goes forward so nobly, that, in few months, before he half knows the needfull Philosophy, he is found to be a Master of Arts in Villany. And moreover, the Parents were by some good friends informed, that lately he was acting the domineering student, and being catcht by the watch, was brought into the Court of Guard; but through the extraordinary intercession of his own and some other Doctors, they privately let him go out again.

A little longer time being expired, he sends Post upon Post dunning letters; his quarter of the years out, his Pockets empty, and the Landlady wants mony; besides there are severall other things that he wants, both of Linnen and Woollen; all which things yield an extraordinary Pleasure, especially, if the mony which is sent, without suffring shipwrack, be imploied and laid out for those necessaries.

For some students are so deeply learnt, that they consume the monies they get in mirth and jovialty, and leave their Landladies, Booksellers, Tailors, Shoomakers, and all whom they are indebted to, unpaid. Nay, his own Cousin, that studied at Cambridge, knew very learnedly how to make a cleaver dispatch, with his Pot-Companions, at Gutterlane, of all the mony that was sent him by his Parents, for his promotion; and under the covert of many well studied lies desired more.

But who knows, what wonderfull students tricks, before he is half so perfect, your son will have learnt, to make his Father and Mother merry with; for, as I have heard, he hath gotten so much aquaintance, that he hath the Bookseller to be his friend, who sets down the prizes of the Books he delivers, three times as much again as they are worth; and for the overplus, he, with some other students, are bravely merry together.

Yea, he's come so far himself, that he doth, to get mony, know how to sell his best Authors; and sets in place of them some Blocks very neatly cut and coloured like gallant Books. And if any one comes that will lay their hands upon them; he saith immediately, eat, drink, smoke and be merry to your hearts content; but whatsoever you do, touch not my books; for that's as a Medean Law and an inviolable statute in my Chamber; as it doth, to the same purpose, stand written thus before my Chamber of Books:

> *Be jolly, sing, and dance; command me with a look,*
> *One thing I do forbid, you must not touch a Book.*

The old Proverb saith, it must bend well, before it can make a good hook. But it is easie to be perceived by the beginning, what may be expected from the flexibility of this precious twig. O extraordinary and magnificent pleasure for the Parents, when they see that their son, in so short a time, is so damnably advanced! And so much the more, a little while after, there comes one and tells them by word of mouth, that there were several

Schollars, which were playing some antick tricks in the night; and amongst some others both their Son and their Cousin were apprehended, and at this very present sad accusations were brought in against them. In the mean while, the Chancellor, having heard that they are all persons of good Parentage, and that there will be brave greasing in the case, laughs in his fist because such things as those are generally moderated and assopiated by the means and infallible vertue of the correcting finger hearb.

This brings the Parents a fine Bartholomew Baby to play with; and if there ly loosely in a corner a fifty pound bag they will go nigh to see how they may make use of it. And this gives a horrible augmentation to the Pleasures of Marriage! But let them turn it and wind it which way they will, the Parents must go thither, and seek by all means possible according to their ability, to pacific the matter.

As they are upon their journey, they hear in every Town where they come, how debauched and wicked lives the Students leads, not only concerning that which was lately done at Oxford, but at other places also. Which makes them be in no small fear, whether their son, perhaps may not be guilty only of this, but some worser misdemeanor, and is therefore at present clapt up.

Here Master Truetale begins to relate, that lately there were four Students, who for some petulancy, had been at Confession by the Mayor, and he with their vomiting up some Guinies, gave them their absolutions; but they perceiving that hereby their purses were cruelly weakned, and that the return of monies did not come according to expectation, took a resolution to get some revenge of him for it. And he having built a new house, caused it, by a curious Workman, to be neatly painted on the outside: which these four Students seeing, they took a good quantity of Tar, and did so damnably bedawb it, that it looked as if old Nick had been there with his rubbing brush. Which the Mayor seeing in the morning, seemed to be little troubled at it; but said, certainly some body hath done this, that I have taken too little mony of, and therefore in gratitude have, for nothing, thus bepainted my delicately painted house.

But nevertheless the Mayor sends in the evening five or six Spies abroad into those Taverns and Alehouses where the lightest Students generally frequented; who were smoking and drinking there, and amongst other discourses related, how it tickled their fancies, that the covetous Mayor was served such a delicate trik, &c. Whereupon some of them hearing that the action was so much commended, and that the Mayor made no search about it, saies, that was my work with James Smith the Londoner, Jack Dove the Kentishman, and Sanny Clow the Scotch man. Upon this they were all four apprehended in the night, and very cleaverly clapt by the heels, &c.

Hereupon Mistriss Credit, said, There are no such wicked inventers of mischief, as moniless Students; of which we had lately a new example, for some of those Blades wanting mony, were resolved to act this trick, *viz.* Some few daies before there was a malefactor hanged, and one of them between eleven and twelve of the clock at night, gets hard by the Gallows where he hung, and feigned to be the spirit of the malefactor; sometimes appearing, and then again vanishing; in the mean while the rest of his companions, all separate from each other, as if they had been strangers, placed themselves not far from it. Each of them seemed to be frightned, and shewed unto all the passers by that there was the spirit of the malefactor that was executed. This run forward like wild fire, in somuch that the number of the spectators increased abundantly. And whilest every one was so busie in beholding it, the moniless Students were as serious in picking of their Pockets, cutting the silver buttons off their cloaths, which no body perceived, till the Spirit was vanished, and they were gotten home. So did I know, saith Master Mouth, two necessitous Students, who at a Fair-time, observed that a Country man, having sold some commodities that he brought to Market, had received five or six Crown pieces for them; and went amongst the Booths to buy somthing, but feared in the throng one or another might steal them from him; therefore would not trust them in his Pocket, nor with his Purse in the breast of his doublet; but puts them in his mouth; saying, No body I'm sure can take them from thence, and walks into the Booths, there cheapning a hat; in the mean while, one of these Students goes to the very next Booth, buies some pedling thing, and pulling mony out of his Pocket to pay, saith what a pox is the meaning of this? Just now I had several Crown pieces, and now I have nothing; and since that, there hath no body else been near me, but this Country fellow; and begins to catch him by the shoulders; saying, hark ye Squire, I miss several Crown pieces which I had but just now. This so amazed the Country man, that he began to mumble with the Crown pieces in his mouth; whereupon the

Student said, I verily beleeve the villain hath them in his mouth. The Country man answered thereupon, those that I have in my mouth are my own, I received them just now for some commodities; But let the Country man say what he would, it was not beleeved; he was lamentably beaten, his Crown pieces taken from him, and given to the Student.

By this you may perceive, saith Master Otherway, that the Proverb is true, *Poverty is subtle.* I was lately told of some poor troublesom Students, who had, a little way off the City, caused a dainty Feast to be made ready for them; and knowing that the Landlord had a brother, whom he extreamly loved, which lived about five and twenty miles off; write a Letter to the Landlord, and therein acquaint him that his Brother was very desperately sick, oftentimes calling for him; therefore if he would see and speak with him alive, he must with all possible speed immediately come thither, &c.

Then they found out such a cleaver contryvance to have this Letter delivered into the hands of the Landlord, that he had not the least distrust of a cheat; but away he rides immediately. In the mean while, these Students committed much sauciness and wantonness with the Mistriss and the Maid; till at last locking them both up in a Chamber, away they went without paying.

To this a Miller that sate close by, relates, that lately, not far from his house, two Students laid violent hands upon a woman, and bound her to a Post.

'Tis a Wonder, saith Master Demure, proceeding forward, that since they commit such wicked and so many base actions, more of these Students are not apprehended. When I dwelt at my Country house, there came a parcel of these drunken blades, that were expresly gone abroad to play some mad tricks; they pulled down the pales of my neighbors Garden; and one among them that served for Chief, commanded pull off these planks, tear up this Post, &c.

In the mean time, a poor Country man coming by with his empty Wagon; begs of this commander, that he would be pleased to bestow upon him those old Planks and Posts for his winter firing, because he was so poor, that he knew not where to get any: which this Gentleman granting him, he laies on a lusty load upon his Wagon.

Being drove a pretty way of, the owner comes to the place, and sees in what a lamentable condition his Garden lay; asks who had done it, and understands that they were Students which had taken their march towards some of the adjacent Country Towns, but that the Country man with his Planks, must needs be got very far from the City, &c. Away runs the owner with all speed, makes his complaint, and gets an order to arrest the poor Country man, his horse and Wagon. Who coming to be examined at his triall, was condemned to be set in the Pillory, with two Planks set before him, upon which must be written in great white Letters.

Garden-Theef.

These wicked Students stood together to behold this, and laught till they split, to see that this poor innocent Country man, must suffer such shame and punishment for his winter firing.

Just in the same manner, not long ago, some divellish Students, had taken a heavy rail from before a house which was newly set there, but hearing that the Watch or Bell man approched; they presently whept it before another mans dore, where there was none; and leaning all of them over the rail; saluted the Watch with saying, Good night Gentlemen, Good night; and the Watch the like to them again: But the Watch was no sooner gone then they fell to breaking of it all in peeces, and run away as fast as they could drive.

Those people are unhappy, saith Master Talkon, especially such as live in Country Towns, that are near to Cities where there are Universities; for many times one or another must be a sufferer from these roguish natured Students; and they imagine in themselves that all what the Country people possess must be at their pleasure and disposition. Whereby it happens, in the Summer, that for their wicked pastime, they go to rob the Orchards of the best fruit, and to steal Hens, Ducks, and Pigeons; and then again to destroy the Fields of Turnips, Carrots, Parsnips, Beans and Pease, &c. Tearing up such multiplicities, that it would be incredible if we should relate it all. But it is common for them to destroy ten times as much as they can eat or carry away.

And when the Summer is past, that there are no fruits either in Orchards or Fields; then their whole delight and recreation is to commit insolencies in the Streets of the City by night; and if they can but any waies put an affront upon the Watch; that is laught at, and esteemed to be an heroick act.

It hapned lately, that some Students walking out of Town, saw a little boy in the Fields, that was holding the cord of an indifferent Kite, which was in the Air, in his hand; they laughing at him, said, The Kite is bigger than the Boy; come let us ty the cord about the Boy, then they will not lose one another. And immediately catching hold of the Boy, they forced the cord from him, and bound it fast about his middle in a great many knots, then went their way.

Whilest the Boy was very busie and indeavouring to unty the knots, the Wind grew high, insomuch that the Boy used all his strength to hold back the cord; but his strength failing him, he was with a furious blast snatcht up by the Kite from the ground, and presently after let fall again into a pretty deep ditch, where the poor innocent Boy was unhappily drowned.

It would be sempiternal for us here to make a relation of all the petulancy and wickedness of Students, whereof these and other Parents, each in their particular, are miserably sensible of. For every one acts his own part, but it tends altogether unto wickedness, lavishness, and troublesomness.

Here you may see Master Empty-belly takes the greatest delight in the World, nobly to treat some Northern Gentlemen of his acquaintance and Pot-companions, and then again to be treated by them: where there is an absolute agreement made, that when any one of them gets mony from their Parents, he shall give the company a treat of five Guinnies. And though they generally observe, that before they part, one quarrel or other arises, and the Swords drawn; yet this Law is inviolabler, than ever any Statutes of Henry the VIII. were. Which continued so long till one of them be desperately wounded or killed, and he that did it apprehended; and to the great greef of his Parents tried for his life, or else flies his Country, to save it.

Others we may see, that have no greater pleasure then to sit whole nights with their Companions playing at Tables; and there game away Rings, Hats, Cloaks and Swords, &c. and then ply one another so close with whole bumpers of Sack and old Hock, that they are worse then senceless beasts, feeling and groping of the very Walls, and tumbling and wallowing to and fro in their own nastiness. And esteem it to be a Championlike action if one can but make the t'other dead drunk by his voracity of sucking in most. As if they intended hereby to become learned Doctors.

Some again are most horribly addicted to frequent the pestilential Bawdy-houses; of which they are never satisfied, till mony, cloaths, books, and their own health of body is consumed; and then come home to their Parents soundly peppered.

Some there are that oftentimes so deeply ingage themselves with their Landlords daughters, that they can answer to her examination without the knowledge either of their Parents or Doctors, and are fit for promotion in the Art of Nature. But if the Landlady hath never a daughter of her own, there's a Neece or Neighbors daughter, which knows how to shew her self there so neatly, that with her tripping and mincing she makes signals enough, that at their house Cubicula locanda is to be had. And these are the true Divers, that know infinitely well how to empty the Students Pockets.

Thus doth every one act their parts. Whilest the Parents are indeavouring to gather and scrape all together that they can, that their Son, who is many times the onliest or eldest, may go forward in his study, and become perfect in one Faculty. And the more, because they see that he is sharp-witted, and according as his Doctor saith, a very hopefull young man. Little thinking that he makes as bad use of those natural benefits, as he is lavish of his mony.

But it is a common saying that the London-youths must have their wills. Which oftentimes occasions, that when they have studied a long time in Divinity, they finally turn to be some Inns of Court Gentlemen; fearing that their wild Students life, might in any other vocation, be cast in their teeth.

Yet somtimes it also happens, that from the very first they behave themselves modestly, and advance so gallantly in their Studies, that it is a comfort for their Parents, and great benefit for themselves. But nevertheless, though they obtain their Promotion with commendation, reputation, and great charges; yet it is all but fastidious, unless their Parents can leave or give them some considerable means; or that they through their brave behaviours, perfections, and sweet discourses, can inveagle themselves in to a rich match. For many years are spent before they can get a Parsonage or Benefice, and when it doth happen in some Country Town, the means will hardly maintain them.

If he be a Counsellor or Doctor of Physick, what a deal of time runs away before he can come in to practice! especially if in the one he hath not the good fortune to get the two or three first causes for his Clients; and in the other, not to make satisfactory cures of his first Patients. Therefore, what a joy would it have been for the Parents if their Son had spent his time in understanding Shop-keeping, and been obedient to the exhortations of his Parents!

But though some do this, and are therein compliant to their Parents; yet we perceive that this also is subject to many vexations, by reason that the children through a contrary drift, many times disturb their Parents night rest; especially when there are such kind of Maids in the house, that will listen to their humors and fancies.

These will, for the most part, please their Master and Mistriss to the full; and do all things so that their Mistriss shall be satisfied, and have no occasion to look out for another: And yet, in the mean while, all their main aim is, to get and intice the son, with their neatness, cleanliness, friendliness, and gentleness, to be on their side. To that end knowing how, as well as their Mistriss, to Hood themselves, curl their locks, and wantonly overspread their breasts with a peece of fine Lawn, or Cambrick, that they seem rather to be finically over shadowed then covered, and may the better allure the weak eys of the beholders.

These know that Dame Nature hath placed her best features in a City Maid, as well as in a Lady at Court: And that there are no keener Swords, or stronger steels to penetrate through the hearts of men, then the handsom bodiedness, comly and kind behaviour of women.

This is oftentimes the occasion that the son hath more inclination towards her, then he hath for a Gentlewoman of a good family and indifferent fortune; nay it transports him so, that they finally make use of one bed; and the son (much unexpected by the Parents) is come to be Father himself. But what an inestimable Pleasure of Marriage this is for the new Grandfather and Grandmother, every one may judge. Especially, if it happens, as I saw once, that the Prentice lay with his Masters Daughter; and the Son with the

Kitchin Wench; and the Prentice run away with the daughter; and the Son would by all means marry with the Kitchin Wench. Which was such a great grief for the Parents, that it might be justly termed rather one of the Terrors than Pleasures of Marriage. So that we see, although the Children be at home by their Parents, or in the shop, and remain under their view and tuition; yet nevertheless, by one or other, never to be expected, occasion, they fall in to evill courses; which every one that brings up children hath such manifold and several waies experience of, that it would be infinite and too tiresom to give you an account of all the Confessions. Therefore we will pass by these (as if we were running a horse-race), and to shorten our journy, return again to our well married Couple, from whom we are cruelly straied.

You see and observe then, O well married Couple, what strange tricks and actions that children will play. If yours act then the part of a liberal Son, or wanton Student, rejoice therein that you have not brought forth a dunce or blockhead; but since his Doctor saith that he is sharp-witted, and a hopefull youth; doubt not, but that you will, when he comes to his seriouser years, with delight and pleasure see him to be a great man.

For it hath many times hapned, that those who have been the maddest and wildest Students at the University, have afterwards come to be noble Personages, Ministers of State, and learned Doctors. Of whom we could relate unto you several examples, if we knew certainly that the revealing of that Confession would not be ill taken.

Thrice happy are you, O noble Couple, that you are yet in possession of the Pleasures of the first Marriage, and are not troubled with the contention of a cross-graind Father-in-law, or Mother-in-law over your Children, nor with their fore-children, or Children of the second bed. For whatsoever happens to you now, comes from a Web of your own spinning, and your love to that, conquers and covers all infirmities; because we know very well that that certainly compleats one of the Pleasures of Marriage.

The Ninth Pleasure.

Of base conditioned Maid-servants.

'Tis true, it seems to fall both tart and bitter, when the children take such lavish courses, and get such wild hairs in their nostrils; the sons acting the parts of spendthrifts, and petulant Students, and the Daughters of light Punks; as long as these things remain so, they appear to be but very sober Pleasures of Marriage. But when we perceive, that these thorns being past, the pleasant roses appear, and that these light hearted Students finally come to be gallant Practitioners; O that affords you the most satisfactory and largest Pleasure of Marriage that ever could be expected.

So also, if you perceive that your Daughters are lively, active and airy; that somtimes they would rather go to a Play, then to Church; or rather be merry of an evening, than at Sermon in the morning, and grow to be altogether mannish minded; you must then conclude these are natural instincts. If it happen to fall out, contrary to your expectation, that she hath more mind to a brave young fellow that's a Prentice, whose parts and humor she knows, then she hath in a Plush Jacketted or gilt Midas; then make your selves joyfull in the several examples that you have of others, who being so married, have proved to be the best Matches; of which examples multiplicities are at large prostrated to your view in the Theater of Lovers. So that you do herein yet find the Pleasure of Marriage.

But it is much farther to be sought for among the vexations which house-keeping people have not only from children, but from base-natured, lasie, tailing, lavish, and ill-tongued servants; done unto them somtimes by their men, but generally by the foolish and stifnecked Maids. These can make their Master totally forget his Base Viol and singing of musick, and their Mistriss the playing upon the Virginals. It was a much less trouble for Arion and Orfeus to charm all the senceless creatures both of Sea and Land in those daies; then it is now for house-keepers to bring their servants to a due obedience.

Neither is this strange, because some Maids, when they see they have gotten a kind natured and mild Gentlewoman to their Mistriss; immediately practice, by all means possible, to rule and domineer over her; insomuch that whatsoever the Mistriss orders or commands, she knows how, according to the imagination of her own understanding, to order and do it otherwise. And dare many times boldly contradict them, and say, *Mistriss, it would be better if this were done then, and that so.*

And if the Mistriss be so mild that she condescends and passes by this some times; they are immediately, in their own conceits, as wise again as their Mistriss; and dare, when they come among their tailing Gossips, brag that they can bend their Mistriss to their Bow; and if their Mistriss bids them do any thing, they do it when it pleases them, or at their own oportunity; for their Mistriss is troubled with the simples, a Sugar-sop, &c.

But if it happen so that one of these Rule-sick Wenches, comes into a service where the Mistriss is a notable spirited woman that looks sharply and circumspectly to the government of her Family, then she's damnably put to't; and is troubled in spirit, that her Mistriss will not understand it so, as she would fain have it, according to her hair-brain'd manner, and gets this to an answer, *Jane, do it as I command you, then it is well, though it were ill done. Let your Mistriss command, its your duty to obey; or else, next time you must hire your self out for Mistriss, and not for Maid, &c.*

How pleasant this answer was to Jane, it appears, because she no sooner gets out, but she runs to Goody Busie-body that hires out servants; where she makes no smal complaint of her Mistresses insulting spirit; and asks whether she knows not of a hire for her by some houskeeping Batchelor or Widower; because she understands the ordring of her work very well, is a special good Cook, and loves Children, &c. Then she would leave her Mistriss, and tell her that her Aunt was very sick and lay a dying, and that she must go thither, &c.

Goody Busie-body is presently ready, because she sees here is a means to earn double wages, the Maid must be provided with another service, and the Mistriss with another Maid; so she begins, like a Broker, to turn and wind it about every way to rid her self of the one, and then to recommend another in the place. Though it be mighty inconvenient for the Mistriss, and troubles her, because she many times may be near her lying-in, or some other pressing necessity, &c.

Whose merrier then Jane, for she hath gotten a new service by a Widower, and can order and govern all things now according to her own mind; where she hath not the name of a Maid, but of a Governantess. Nay, now she's cunning enough to bridle in all her ill conditions, and watches the very ey of her Master, keeping all things very cleanly and neat in order; upon hopes that her Master might fall into a good humour, and make a place also for her in his bed. For verily she loves Children so well that she would be helping to get one her self. To which purpose she useth all inventions imaginable, running too and again about the house bare-necked, and her breasts raised up; or comes to his bedside all unlaced, or fains to sit sleeping by the fire side with her coats up to her knees, against her Master comes home, with the key in his Pocket, merrily disposed, from his Companions; or with a short Coat on, stoops down very low in the presence of her Master, to take up somthing from, or clean the flore; or climbs up a ladder to rub the glass windows; and knows of a thousand such manner of inticements, of which there's never a one of them, but, if the Master have any flesh or blood in him, are sufficient to catch and insnare him. For this hapned to her fellow Creature who having dwelt some indifferent time with a Widower, he came home one evening pretty merry, and jestingly talked to her about her sweetheart; *See there, Peggy, be carefull, and when you come to marry, I will give you this bed that I ly on, with all that belongs to it.* Whereupon the Maid answered, *Well Sir, if I shall have all that justly belongs to it, I must have you also Sir, for it is yours, and you ly upon it.* The answer pleased the Master so well, that he catches Peggy in his arms, throws her upon the bed, and lies down by her; till at last, in spite of all his relations, he made his Maid his Wife: who being married, then began to discover her stifnecked, cross-graind humors, that she had so long kept secret; but it was the occasion of both their ruines.

But we will leave Jane and Peggy with their Widowers, and take a view what kind of a Pleasure of marriage that our Mistriss possesseth with her new Maid; for Goody Busie-body recommended her highly to be a very honest, vertuous Maid, of a good family, and gave her self security for her fidelity.

Nevertheless, there are hardly three daies past, but the Mistriss perceives that she is notably inclined to toss up her cup: but for the better certainty, the Mistriss commands her to draw some Wine in a glass that was very clean rinsed; which she no sooner brought back, but the Mistriss observed that greasy lips had been at it; yet before she sent her the second time, she takes a trencher and holds it over the smoke of a Candle to grow black, then with her finger rubs that soot upon the edge or hollow part of the glass; and commanded her, as she did before, to draw some Wine; but when she came back again, the Mistriss then perceived that the round circle of the glass was impressed upon both sides of her mouth and upon her forehead. Who can abstain themselves from laughter, when they see such a marked sheep come out of the Wine Cellar? Who could imagine that a Maid in three daies time should occasion so much pleasure of marriage! How much more mirth will you receive from her, when she has taken a good bowsing cup to be jolly! You have here a triall of her fidelity, that Goody Busie-body vaunted of. For the future she may very well say, that she is mighty dexterous at smuckling of Wine; who knows but she may get an Angel a year the more wages for it.

But whilest she pleases her Mistriss with this sight, the t'other causes her to enjoy a new recreation: for she having gotten leave to go to Church in th'afternoon, tarries out till seven of the clock in the evening, tho she knows there are friends invited to supper, the children must be got to bed, and all things set in good order; neither is it strange, for she thinks, I am now the eldest Maid, the t'other may attend. When I hired my self, my Mistriss told me I should go on Sundaies to Church; and also, when occasion served, after Sermon I should walk abroad for an hour or two; and now there is a very good opportunity, because she hath another Maid at home, &c.

She keeps singing in this tune. And finally coming home, thinks that she has a great deal of reason on her side, and is not ashamed to retort ten cross words for one. 't Is no wonder neither, for she had been talking with Mistriss Sayall the Cupster, who had Cupt her but the Sunday before, and then told her that she could observe out of her physiognomy, and the course of her blood, several infallible signs, that she should come to be a woman of good quality, and that she would not be above a year unmarried. Also there came thither at the same time Dorothy and Margery, whom Mistriss Sayall had in like manner prognosticated what was befallen them. These did not a little admire, that she, being now the eldest Maid, earned such small wages, and that her Mistriss did not raise it; because she deserved at the least fifteen shillings a year more, and a better New years gift, and Fairing.

Thus they stuff one anothers pates full. And Mistriss Sayall, and Goody Busiebody, seem to be as if they were sisters cast in one Mould; for the one knows how to blow the simple wenches ears full; and the t'other, worse then a Bawd, makes them cross-grain'd; and keep both of them a school for ill-natured Wenches, and lazy sluts, to natter, to exhort, and to exasperate in; yet these half Divel-drivers, carry themselves before the Mistresses like Saints; but do indeed, shew themselves to be the most deceitfullest cheats, who carry alwaies fire in one hand and water in the t'other.

These know how, very subtlely, many times, to fatten their carkasses, with meat and drink out of the Mistresses Cellars and Butteries; keeping alwaies a fair correspondence with the theevish Maids, which know many tricks and waies how to convey it unto them; and scold and brawl against those whose stoln meat and drink they thus idly and basely convey away. These use again all possible indeavours to recommend them here or there to a sweetheart, and make their own houses serve as an Exchange for this Negotiation; where they appear as precise at their hours, as a Merchant doth at Change-time.

This it is, that makes them look like a Dog in a halter, when they cannot get leave on Sundaies to go a gadding; and it is a wonder they do not bargain for it when they hire themselves: though there are some that are not ashamed, (who dare not so openly confess this) to bargain that they may go every Sunday to Church, as if they were extraordinary devout, when it is really to no other end, then to set out their gins, to catch some Tailor, Baker, Shoomaker, Cooper, Carpenter, Mason, or such like journyman: which is hardly passed by to satisfie their fleshly lusts, before they perceive that they have chosen a poor and wretched for a plentifull livelihood; and are often, by their husbands, beaten like Stockfish, though Lent be long past. But what delight they have, in being curried with this sort of five-tooth'd Comb, the neighbours can judge by the miserable songs they sing.

These find also the Pleasures of Marriage, at which they have so long aimed, and so much indeavoured for; and would now gladly lick their fingers at that which they have many times thrown away upon the

Dunghills, or in the Kennels; falling many times into deplorable poverty, or to receive Alms from the Churchwardens and charitable people; of which there are vast numbers of examples, too lamentable and terrible to be related.

By this small relation you may see what kind of points these sort of people have upon their Compass. But to write the true nature and actions of such Rubbish, were to no other purpose then to foul a vast quantity of paper with a deal of trash and trumpery. For many are damnably liquorish tooth'd, everlasting Tattlesters, lazy Ey-servants, salt Bitches, continual Mumblers out of their Pockets, wicked Scolds, lavish Drones, secret Drinckers, stifnecked Dunces, Tyrants over Children, Stinking Sluts, Mouldy Brain'd trugs; hellish sottish Gipsies; nay and sometimes both Whorish and Theevish; and must, therefore, not have come into consideration here, if they did not so especially belong to the disconsolations of Marriage; occasioning many times more troubles and disquiets in a Family, then all the rest of the adversities that may befall it.

This is the reason that makes the Mistriss many times turn one after t'other out of dores; and is afreard that a new one should come in again. And is also ashamed that the Neighbors should see every foot a new Maid upon her flore; who by an evil nature, are ready to beleeve the worst of their fellow neighbours, what is told them by a tale-carrying, long-tongued Slut of a Maid; though they many times observe how wickedly they are plagued with their own.

O super-excellent Pleasure of Marriage! where shall we make a conclusion, if we should set all things down according to their worth and value! Certainly every one would, to that purpose, want a Clark in their own Family.

The Tenth Pleasure.

An empty Purse, makes a sorrowfull Pate. The Husband grows jealous. And the Wife also. The Husband is weary of his wife, and seeks to be divorced.

As continual prosperity giveth a great satisfaction to married people; and congealeth their hearts more and more with a fervent Love; so, on the contrary, we many times see, that when they are oppressed with bad Trading, Bankrupts, chargeable housekeeping and Children, it occasions and raises a coolness in the affections; insomuch that it disquiets their rest, and they consume the whole night many times with flying fancies and cogitations, how such an Assignment, or that Bill of Exchange, or the last half years rent shal be paid, &c. because the emptness of their Purse, and the slow paiment of their Debtors too much impedes them. And their yearly rents are so small and uncertain, that there runs away many times more in reparations and taxations annually then the rents amounts to. This occasions disquiet. From this it proceeds, that many times when they rise, their wits run a wool-gathering, and they are more inclined to look crabbedly, grumble and mumble, then to shew each other any signs of love and friendship: for an empty purse, makes a sorrowfull pate. This gives no smal defeat to the Pleasures of Marriage. Now they begin to observe that there is no state or condition in the World so compleat, but it hath some kind of imperficiency.

Published by the Navarre Society, London.

This kind of necessity may, by a man, in a Tavern, with good company, be rinsed with a glass of Wine, but never thereby be supplied: And the woman may with singing and dandling of her children, or controuling and commanding of her servants, a little forget it, yet nevertheless when John the cashier comes with the Bill of Exchange, and William the Bookkeeper with the Assignment, they ought both to be paid, or else credit and respect ly at the stake. This requires a great deal of prudence, to take care for the one, and preserve the other.

The best sort of Matches have found this by experience to be true: And for that reason they ofttimes stop a little hole to make a bigger. But because this can be of no long continuance, some do measure their business smaller out at first, and dwell at a lesser rent, hire out their Chambers and Cellars; and afterwards, make mony of some movables, will not turmoil themselves with so much trade, and great trust; nay sometimes also, take some other trade by the hand, the commodities whereof are of a quicker consumption. And if this happen to people that are not so perfectly well match'd, as our self-same-minded couple, and that the husband hath been a frequenter of company, you shall then seldom see that the husband and the Wife are concordant in their opinions; for he generally will be for trading in Wine and Tobacco, in which sort of commodities he is well studied; and the woman is for dealing in linnen, stockings, gloves, or such like Wares as she knows best how to traffick with. And verily it looks but sadly (although it oftentimes happens) when a Man and his Wife do contend about this. Nevertheless some men, because they imagine to have the best understanding, use herein a very hard way of discourse with their wives, making it all their business to snap and snarl, chide and bawl, nay threaten and strike also; which indeed rather mars then mends the matter, little thinking that quietness in a family is such a costly Jewell, that it seldom can be valued.

Others, on the contrary, take their greatest delight, when they know how, with affableness to please their wives humour, and with plausible words can admonish them what is best and fittest to be done; and rather to extoll those graces which are found in them, than to reprove their deficiencies: According to the instructions of the prudent Emperor Marcus Aurelius, who said, that men ought often to admonish their wives, seldom reprove them, and never strike them.

But many men whose understanding is turned topsie turvy in their brains, seek it in a contrary place, and where the Bank is lowest, the Water breaks in soonest. In such case the Women suffer cruelly. For if he be foul-mouth'd, he is not ashamed openly before his servants and other people to check, curb, and controul his wife lustily; and when they are in private together, reprehends her so bitterly, that he would not dare to mention it in the ears of honest people: because having seen that his Border, out of meer civility, cut many times the best peece at Table and presented to his Wife, bilds thereupon a foundation of jealousie, and an undoubted familiarity, which he privately twits her in the teeth with; though in publick he is ashamed to let it appear that he is jealous; because then he would be laught at for it; therefore he doth nothing but pout, mumble, bawl, scold, is cross-grain'd and troubled at every thing; nay looks upon his Wife and all the rest of his Family like a Welsh Goat, none of them knowing the least reason in the World for it.

In the meanwhile he useth all possible means privately to attrap his wife; for to see that which he never will see; and at which he is so divellishly possessed to have a wicked revenge; nay which he also never can see though he had a whole boxfull of spectacles upon his nose; because she never hath, or ever will give him the least reason for it. In that manner violating loves knot, and laying a foundation of implacable hatred.

Verily, if a woman be a little light-hearted and merry humoured, it is a great delight and pleasure for her to be taking notice, and every way to be scoffing, with all the foolish tricks and devices of such a jealous Coxcomb. But otherwise there is no greater Hell upon Earth, then for an honest Woman to dwell with a jealous husband; because in his absence she dare not in the least speak to any one, and in his presence hardly look upon any body. This is known to those, who have had experience of it, and it never went well with any Family where this damned house-divel ever got an entrance.

'Tis true, all men are not defiled with this dirtiness. But such Loggerheads many times occasion, through their wicked folly and evil doings, that the Woman, who before never thought of jealousie, now begins to grow jealous her self. For she, considering that her husband is so without any ground or reason, looks so sour, and ill-natured; and alwaies when he comes home every thing stands in his way; besides, that the soothings and friendly entertainments, should differ so much from those of former times, and especially from them of the first year; cannot imagine that the small gain and the bad times are the occasion of it; therefore she thinks that there is some other fine Gipsie, that puts him on to these base humors, or that he is led away by some or other charming Punk.

And it is no wonder, because coming home lately he said, that somewhere as he was walking home he had lost his Watch, which he had just as he was coming out of the Tavern. And two or three weeks before came home without his Cloak, saying, that some wicked Rascals had taken it from him in the streets. Moreover she rememorates, how he related not long since, that he had been, out of jest, one evening, with three or four others, in six of the most vile and wickedest Bawdy houses in the City, though that he had committed nothing unhandsom there, as he said; therefore she thinks that she hath more reason to suspect his evil doings, then he hath of hers.

And having pondered upon all these things, this and t'other way, imagineth that she hath a great deal of reason to suspect him. Nay, the daily grumbling and mumbling, the lessening of the mony, his coming home late at nights, his cool kindness, besides all the rest, seem to be sufficient proofs. So that here the Pleasure of Marriage is so monstrously Clouded, as if there were a great Eclipse of the Sun, and it will be a wonder to see with what kind of colour it will appear again. For the Husband catechizes his Wife with such a loud voice, that it is generally heard through the whole neighbourhood; and the Wife, to vindicate her innocency, lets fly at him again with such a shrill note, as if she had gone to school to learn it in Drury Lane, or Turnball street. And it is a wonder that the first Chyrurgian is not sent for to cure this Woman of her bad tongue.

Here you ought to come, O restless Lovers, to behold your selves in these two darlings; you, who in your wooing are also possessed with jealousie, if you see that another obtains access to your Mistriss; or who, perhaps as wel as you, doth but once kiss the knocker of the dore, or cause an Aubade to be plaied under her Chamber Window: Look sharply about you, and behold how these Aubades decline, or whether it be worth your while to give your Rival the Challenge; or to stab, poison, or drown'd your self, to shew, by such an untimely death, the love you had for her; and on your Grave, bear this Epitaph, that through damn'd jealousie you murthered your self. These married Couple, used to do so; but see now what a sad life they live together, because jealousie took root in them so soon, and now bringeth forth such evill fruits.

Oh that this, now senceless, married Couple, had here, like the Athenians, prudent Umpires! how easily might they, perhaps, be united and pacified!

For the Athenians had constituted a certain sort of superiors, whom they intituled Pacificators of the married people; whose Power was to appease all differences between married people; and to constrain them that they must live in peace and unity with each other. In like manner at Rome a Temple was built, where scolding married people, being reunited, came to sacrifice, and to live in better tranquility.

But alas! it is now clear contrary, such contentious Couples, use all the means and indeavours they possibly can rather to be divorced, then reunited; to that end solliciting both the Majestical and Ecclesiastical Powers; to whom are related a thousand sad reasons by each party, because either of them pretendeth to have the greatest reason on their side; of which this Age imparteth us several examples, wherewith the Magistracy, Ministry and Elders find no small trouble; especially, if they be people of a brave extraction, good credit and reputation, who have procreated severall children together. For this jealous and contentious house Divell, domineers as well among people of great respect, as those of lesser degree; though there be some which so order it, that they smother this fire within dores, and suffer it not to burst out at the house top. Nevertheless it is impossible to hide this unkindness from the eys of them that are in the Family. Therefore it is to be admired, that the sister who dwelleth with this married Couple, and seeth and hears all this unkindness, mumbling and grumbling, yet hath such an earnest desire to be set down in the List of the great Company. Nay though she had read all the twenty Pleasures of Marriage through and through, and finds by the example of her Brother that they are all truth; yet she is like a Fish, never at rest till she gets her self into the Marriage-Net, where she knows that she never can get out again: According to these following Verses, which she hath sung so many times:

> *You may in sea lanch when you will,*
>   *To see the boistrous Main,*
> *Great storms, and wind, your sails will fill,*
>   *Fore you return again.*
> *The married state, is much like this,*
>   *O'rewhelm'd with many crosses,*
> *Yet must be born, see how it is,*
>   *With tauntings, toils, and losses.*

But I beleeve that the Sister makes flesh and blood her Counsellors, just as her Brother did, who hath now totally forgotten these Verses; for since the flesh is almost come to the very bone, all his designs and indeavours seem to bend now to the being separated from Bed and Table: and, if fortune would favour it, he would rather see it done by death, then any Civil Authority; for then he might look out again for a new Beloved, and by that means get another new Portion; though it might lightly happen to be some mendicant hous-divel, for a reward of his jealousie.

And perhaps he little thinks how that bawling and scolding, between him and his Wife, is spread abroad. But it hath often hapned, that those who would be separated, very unexpectedly have been parted by death; but not so neither, that they who most desired the separation, have just remained alive.

Happy were those restless Souls, if they did like the wise and prudent Chyrurgians, who will not cut off any member, before they have made an operation of all imaginable means for cure and recovery thereof: And that they first learnt to know their own deficiences perfectly, that they might the better excuse those of their Adversary.

O how thrice happy are our well-matcht Couple! who like a Looking-glass for all others, live together in love, pleasure and tranquility, and have banished that monstrous beast jealousie out of their hearts and house; wishing nothing more then to live long together, and to dy both at one time, that neither of them both might inherit that grief to be the longest liver, by missing their second-selves. These do recommend marriage in the highest degree to the whole World, as the noblest state and condition; and despise the folly of those who reject it, imagining in themselves that they have more knowledge and understanding then all the wise men of Greece ever had; who by their marrying demonstrated, that they esteemed the married estate to be the best and commendablest though some of them were married to women, who notably bore the sway.

We may very well then contemn the chattering of Epicurus that pleasurable Hoggrubber, who said, that no wise man would ever give himself in to the Bands of Matrimony; because there is so much grief, trouble, and misery to be found in it. For we see to the contrary, that the Wise men long to be in it, and that the Sun of understanding appears more gloriously in them, when it is nourisht and inlivened by marriage; especially, if they have got, like unto our well-married Couple, good Matches. To this end, all those that are unmarried, ought to look very circumspectly, for the getting themselves such a second-self, that they would never desire to part with. And for the exhortation of every one to this, I will break off and conclude with that faithfull warning given by that great Emperor and Philosopher Marcus Aurelius: saying, *Because the life of Man cannot remain without Women, I do warn the young, pray the old, admonish the wise, and teach the simple, that they should shun ill-natured Women as much as the Plague: for I say, that all the venemous Creatures in the World, have not so much poison spread or contained in their whole bodies; as one divellish-natured Woman alone hath in her tongue.*

The End

www.ingramcontent.com/pod-product-compliance
Lightning Source LLC
Chambersburg PA
CBHW081156020426
42333CB00020B/2528